WE WANTED
TO BE FREE

*

By the author of

HOLIDAY ROUNDUP
WE CAME TO AMERICA

AN ANTHOLOGY
Introduced and edited by
FRANCES CAVANAH

WE WANTED TO BE FREE

The Refugees'
Own Stories

* ** *

MACRAE SMITH COMPANY
Philadelphia

7109

5-31-72

ACKNOWLEDGMENTS
The editor and publishers wish to express their appreciation for permission to reprint material copyrighted or otherwise controlled to:

FREDERICK G. BROWNELL, for quotation from "Thank You, America," by Alexander Washchenko, as told to Frederick G. Brownell. From the August 1955 issue of *The American Magazine.*

E.P. DUTTON & CO., INC., for "Conversation With Pablo Casals" from the book *Conversations With Casals* by J. Ma. Corredor, Trans. by André Mangeot. Copyright, ©, 1956 by E.P. Dutton & Co., Inc., publishers, and reprinted with their permission.

GAMBIT, INCORPORATED., for "House Arrest," an excerpt from the book *House Arrest* by Helen Vlachos. Copyright, Gambit, 1970. Reprinted by permission of the publisher.

HARCOURT BRACE JOVANOVICH, INC., for "How We Like America," condensed and adapted from *Thank You Twice* by Carolyn and Eddie Bell, edited by Alden Hatch, copyright, 1941, by Harcourt Brace Jovanovich, Inc.; renewed 1969, by Alden Hatch. Reprinted by permission of the publishers.

HARPER & ROW, PUBLISHERS, INC., for "I Belong to Myself," abridged and adapted from pp. 138–169 in *Eighth Moon* by Sansan as told to Bette Lord. Copyright © 1964 by Bette Lord. Reprinted by permission of Harper & Row, Publishers, Inc.

HOUGHTON MIFFLIN COMPANY, for "Mine Eyes Beheld the Promised Land" abridged from *The Promised Land* by Mary Antin. Copyright 1940 by Mary Antin. Reprinted by permission of the publisher, Houghton Mifflin Company. ——for "Rescue" from *The Story of a Secret State*. Copyright, 1944, by Jan Karski. Reprinted by permission of the publisher, Houghton Mifflin Company.

LIFE, for "The Deliverance of Sister Cecelia" from "The Deliverance of Sister Cecilia," *Life Magazine,* May 17, 1954, © 1954 Time Inc. ——for "My Escape from Norway" from "My Escape from Norway," June 10, 1940, © *Life Magazine,* June 10, 1940 Time Inc.

J. B. LIPPINCOTT COMPANY, for "The First Ten Years Are the Hardest," slightly abridged from the book *The Story of the Trapp Family Singers* by Maria Augusta Trapp. Copyright, 1949, by Maria Augusta Trapp. Reprinted by permission of J. B. Lippincott Company.

GEORGE M. MARDIKIAN, For "My Armenia—My America," condensed from *Song of America,* © 1956 by George M. Mardikian. Reprinted by permission of the author.

PALM PUBLISHERS Ltd., Dorval, P.W., Canada, for "This Was My Choice," from the book *This Was My Choice* by Igor Gouzenko—by permission Palm Publishers, Ltd. Copyright 1948.

PRAEGER PUBLISHERS, Inc., for selection from YOU ARE ALL ALONE, by Jozsef Kovago, copyright 1959.

THE READER'S DIGEST, for "Stowaway" by Armando Socarra Ramirez, Denis Fodor and John Reddy. Reprinted with permission from the January 1970 *Reader's Digest.* Copyright 1969 by The Reader's Digest Assn., Inc.

FRED A. SONDERMANN, for "Refugee's Return" by Fred A. Sondermann, from article "September 1939, September 1969" in the summer 1970 issue of *Colorado College Magazine*.

UNIVERSITY OF CHICAGO PRESS, for selection from *Atoms in the Family* by Laura Fermi. Copyright 1954 and reprinted by permission of the University of Chicago Press.

STANLEY YOUNG, for selection from *My Sister and I* by Dirk Van der Heide. Copyright 1941.

This book is dedicated to my niece
MARJORIE CAVANAH SIRACUSA

Contents

*(The dates in parentheses indicate the year
the refugee authors reached their new homes)*

The Refugees Speak
For Themselves

"Prepare in time an asylum for mankind," wrote Thomas Paine in *Common Sense*, the pamphlet urging the colonies to declare their independence. In letters to friends, General George Washington, who was to become the first President of the new nation, also used the word "asylum" and expressed the hope that the "oppressed of the earth" might find "the second land of Promise" in the western lands to be opened up for settlement. The third President, Thomas Jefferson, spoke of the United States as a "sanctuary" for victims of "misrule in Europe."

Since then several of his successors in the White House have popularized such expressions as "a nation of immigrants" and "We are all immigrants or the descendants of immigrants"—enduring phrases that pack much truth into a few words. The amazing story of American progress cannot be separated from the history of immigration. Without the long succession of newcomers to our shores the colonies could never have been settled. Nor could the new nation have expanded across a continent and become the influential giant among other nations that it is today.

Many came for economic reasons: to escape poverty and to give their children a better chance in life than they had ever known. Others fled religious persecution in the Old World. Among those refugees who crossed the oceans seeking freedom in the American colonies was a band of settlers later called Pilgrims, who are said to have stepped from the *Mayflower* onto a little rock still carefully preserved on the beach at Plymouth, Massachusetts. Persecuted French Huguenots and English Catholics came also, and Jews and

Quakers from several European countries. After the United States became a nation, political upheavals in Europe sent thousands of political refugees to our shores, to be followed during our present century by many victims of Fascist, Nazi, and Communist oppression.

One Austrian boy whose family had brought him to the United States after the Nazis imposed their rule on Austria in 1938 was much impressed by the school he attended. One day shortly before Thanksgiving his history class was discussing the Pilgrims. When he learned that they had come in search of freedom, his face brightened.

"Then I am just like the Pilgrims," he said.

Refugees, whether they arrived three centuries ago or in our own time, are all pilgrims and have made special contributions to their adopted land. The following chapters are prefaced by brief summaries of the influence of earlier escapees and exiles—those who sought temporary sanctuary in times of crisis—in shaping our history. Both Josiah Henson and Mary Antin are included, since their influence lives on, but in the main *We Wanted to Be Free* is concerned with men, women, and children who were participants in some of the dramatic events that have shaken the world since World War I.

No one is more entitled to tell the real-life stories of refugees than the refugees themselves. Seeing America through their eyes and realizing what it has meant to them can be a moving experience. Not that any generation of newcomers has ever found an ideal America. They found an America, to quote Carl Schurz, that was "hopefully struggling" toward an ideal. Another escapee who arrived more than a hundred years after Schurz expressed the same idea in these words: "Here, too, men suffer, but they have the right to cry out loud."

Crying out loud—protesting and trying to set right that which is wrong—is an American privilege. It is well to be reminded of this by some to whom it has been denied.

F. C.

WE WANTED
TO BE FREE

*

I

Refugees from the United States

Although the United States has long been the "asylum for mankind" wished for by Thomas Paine, there have been thousands of Americans who sought sanctuary elsewhere. During the American Revolution the Loyalists or Tories, who remained faithful to the mother country, found their situation increasingly uncomfortable after the Treaty of 1783 recognized the independence of the United States. During those difficult years about twenty-five thousand United Empire Loyalists fled from their homes and established themselves in Canada. At that time it was still a pioneer untamed land, and many families in Nova Scotia, New Brunswick, and Ontario today look back with pride on what their ancestors accomplished.

They wielded considerable influence on the history of their adopted country. Before their coming the majority of settlers in Canada spoke French. The influx of English-speaking emigrés from the American Revolution, followed by other waves of immigration from the United States and the British Isles, has made English the dominant language in most parts of Canada today.

Some eighty years after the American Revolution, the defeat of the Confederate States in the American Civil War sent another ten thousand exiles into other countries, many of them to Canada. Some of those new refugees, their farms and businesses ruined by the war, wanted to make a new start elsewhere. Others—officers who had served in the Confederate armies and officials in the Confederate government—left to avoid indictment for treason.

A colony of Confederate exiles was established in the town of Niagara on the Canadian side of the Falls, within sight of United

1

States territory. Across the river the exiles could see the Stars and Stripes flying above Fort Niagara, a constant reminder of the homeland to which some of them did not dare to return. Later, after President Andrew Johnson issued a Universal Amnesty Proclamation on Christmas Day, 1868, many of the exiles did go back. Others, still bitter about the outcome of the war, chose to remain in Canada.

In our own time, differing opinions about the American involvement in Vietnam have divided the citizens of the United States. Though some of them approved their government's decision to aid the government of South Vietnam, others believed the undeclared war to be unconstitutional and morally wrong. A few of the young Americans who protested were unwise and turned to violence, but many more took part in legal and orderly demonstrations. Numbers of young men refused to be drafted to serve in a war which they considered a betrayal of the ideals of the nation's founders.

For such war resisters, two courses were open. They could disobey the law and take the consequences by going to prison. Or they could evade the draft by escaping to another country.

The first alternative was chosen by Robert Eaton, a Quaker whose great-great-grandfather had fled to the United States after taking part in a student demonstration against the militaristic policies of the Prussian government.

"We won't allow militarism to drive us out as my ancestors were driven from Germany," young Eaton told the judge who was about to sentence him to prison. "We're staying because America will be better if there are people willing to work and sacrifice, if necessary, to make it better. . . . I don't want to go to prison. What man does? But it is a risk I take."

Other draft resisters, believing that nothing could be accomplished by going to prison, chose exile. Some members of the armed forces stationed in Europe deserted to Sweden. A few others went there to avoid being drafted, because they were conscientiously opposed to the war.

By far the largest number of draft resisters, those who chose exile but had not yet entered the service, crossed the border into Canada. Often lonely and unhappy, they knew that they could not return to their old homes without risking arrest. Many applied for Canadian citizenship.

Though the draft resisters had disobeyed the law, it was not the first time in American history that men and women had been convinced that a higher law was more important. More than a century ago numbers of leading citizens had refused to abide by the Fugitive Slave Act requiring that runaway slaves be arrested and returned to their former masters. A network of "stations" established in an "underground railroad" enabled thousands of black slaves—the refugees of those times—to reach Canada, where slavery was illegal. They, too, ran grave risks. But they wanted to be free.

One man who helped more than a hundred blacks to escape was Josiah Henson, who had once been a fugitive himself. He was one of the prototypes for the main character in Harriet Beecher Stowe's *Uncle Tom's Cabin*, but he bore little resemblance to the servile "Uncle Tom" that many readers have considered him. After Henson's flight he learned to read, became a Methodist minister, and with the help of white friends organized a successful cooperative venture in the lumber business for the benefit of fugitives in Canada. He lectured in several northern states on behalf of the abolitionist movement, and he gave lectures in England. On one of his trips there to promote his business enterprises, he was invited to Windsor Castle by Queen Victoria and was entertained by such notables as the Prime Minister and the Archbishop of Canterbury.

Though the character of Uncle Tom was a composite picture of several slaves Mrs. Stowe had known, she found her chief inspiration in talking with Josiah Henson and in reading his true story. Unlike the fictitious Uncle Tom, who died a martyr's death, the real man lived to the ripe old age of ninety-four. The following account is condensed from his autobiography.

Escape to Freedom (1830)

BY JOSIAH HENSON

Canada was often spoken of as the only sure refuge from pursuit for slaves trying to escape, and that blessed land was now the desire of my longing heart. Infinite toils and perils lay between me and that haven of promise; but the fire behind me

was too hot and fierce to let me pause to consider them. I knew
the North Star—blessed be God for setting it in the heavens.
I knew it had led thousands of my poor, hunted brethren to
freedom, and had I been concerned for my own safety only, I
would have felt all difficulties light in view of the hope that was
set before me. But, alas! I had a wife and four dear children;
how should I provide for them? Abandon them I could not; not
even for the blessed boon of freedom. They, too, must go.
They, too, must share with me the life of liberty, and I devised
a plan of escape.

But my wife was overwhelmed with terror. She knew nothing of the wide world beyond, and her imagination peopled it
with unseen horrors. We should die in the wilderness, we
should be hunted down with bloodhounds. She was in tears
and she besought me to remain at home. In vain I explained
my master was going to sell me and she and I would be torn
asunder any moment. I talked of the happiness we should
enjoy together in a land of freedom, safe from all pursuing
harm. I argued the matter with her at various times, till I was
satisfied that argument alone would not prevail.

I then told her deliberately that though it would be a cruel
trial for me to part with her, I would nevertheless do it, and
take all the children with me except the youngest, rather than
remain at home, only to be forcibly torn from her. The whole
night long she urged me to relent; exhausted, I left her the
next morning, to go to my work for the day. Before I had gone
far, I heard her calling me, and waiting till I came up, she said,
at last, she would go with me. Blessed relief! my tears of joy
flowed faster than had hers of grief.

Our cabin in Kentucky was near the landing. The plantation
itself extended the whole five miles from the house to the Ohio
River. There were several distant farms, all of which I was
overseeing, and therefore I was riding about from one to another every day. The chief difficulty was connected with the
youngest two of the children. They were of three and two

years, respectively, and of course would have to be carried. I had directed my wife to make me a knapsack of tow cloth, large enough to hold them both, and arranged with strong straps to go around my shoulders. This done, I had practiced carrying them night after night, both to test my own strength and accustom them to submit to it. To them it was fine fun, and I found I could manage them successfully. I resolved to start the next Saturday. Sunday was a holiday; on Monday and Tuesday I was to be away on farms distant from the house; thus several days would elapse before I should be missed.

At length the eventful night arrived. It was about the middle of September, and by nine o'clock all was ready. It was a dark, moonless night when we got into the little skiff in which I had induced a fellow slave to set us across the river. It was an anxious moment. We sat still as death. In the middle of the stream the good fellow said to me, "It will be the end of me if this is ever found out; but you won't be brought back alive, will you?"

"Not if I can help it," I replied.

"But if you get seized, you'll never tell my part in this business?"

"Not if I'm shot through like a sieve."

"That's all," said he, "and God help you."

Heaven rewarded him. He, too, has since followed in my steps; and many a time in a land of freedom have we talked over that dark night on the river.

In due time we landed on the Indiana shore. A grateful farewell, such as none but companions in danger can know, and I heard the oars of the skiff propelling him homeward. There I stood in the darkness, my dear ones with me, and the unknown future before us. But there was little time for reflection. Before daylight came, we must put as many miles behind us as possible and be safely hidden in the woods. We trudged on cautiously and steadily, and as fast as the darkness and the feebleness of my wife and boys would allow. She trembled like a leaf, and even then implored me to return.

For a fortnight we pressed on, keeping to the road during the night, hiding whenever a chance vehicle or horseman was heard, and during the day burying ourselves in the woods. Two days before reaching Cincinnati our provisions were exhausted, and all night long the children cried with hunger. It was a bitter thing to hear them cry, and God knows I needed encouragement myself. My limbs were weary, and my back and shoulders raw with the burden I carried. A dread of detection ever pursued me, and I would start out of my sleep in terror, my heart beating against my ribs, expecting to find the dogs and slave-hunters after me. But now something must be done; it was necessary to run the risk of exposure by daylight upon the road in quest of food.

The only way to proceed was to adopt a bold course. Accordingly, I left our hiding place, took to the road, and turned toward the south, to lull any suspicion that might be aroused were I to be seen going the other way. Before long I came to a house. A furious dog rushed out at me, and his master followed to quiet him. I asked if he would sell me a little bread and meat.

He was a surly fellow. No, he said, he had nothing for niggers!

At the next house I succeeded no better, at first. The man of the house met me in the same style; but his wife, hearing our conversation, said to him, "How can you treat any human being so? We have children, and who knows, they may some day need a friend."

She asked me to come in, loaded a plate with venison and bread, and when I laid it into my handkerchief, and put a quarter on the table, she quietly took it up and put it in my handkerchief, with an additional quantity of venison. I felt the hot tears roll down my cheeks as she said, "God bless you," and I hurried away to my starving wife and little ones.

A little while after eating the venison, which was quite salt, the children became very thirsty. I went off stealthily, breaking the bushes to keep my path, to find water. I found a little rill, and drank a large draught. Then I tried to carry some in my hat; but, alas! it leaked. Finally I took off both shoes, which luckily had no holes in them, rinsed them out, filled them with water, and carried it to my family. They drank with great delight. I have since then sat at splendidly furnished tables in Canada, the United States, and England; but never did I see any human beings relish anything more than my poor famishing little ones did that refreshing draught out of their father's shoes.

That night we made a long run, and two days afterward we reached Cincinnati. On an earlier trip here for my master, I had made friends, and I now felt comparatively at home. Before entering the town I hid my wife and children in the woods, and then walked on alone in search of my friends. They welcomed me warmly, and just after dusk my wife and children were brought in, and we found ourselves hospitably cheered and refreshed. Two weeks of exposure to incessant fatigue, anxiety, rain, and chill made it indescribably sweet to enjoy once more the comfort of rest and shelter. They provided for our welfare until our strength was recruited, and then they set us thirty miles on our way by wagon.

After that, we followed the same course as before—traveling by night and resting by day—till we arrived at the Scioto River in Ohio. We had been told that this far north we might travel safely by day. We found the road but nobody had told us that it was cut through the wilderness, and I had neglected to provide any food, thinking we should soon come to some habitation, where we could be supplied. But we traveled all day without seeing one and lay down at night hungry and weary. The wolves were howling around us, and though they were too cowardly to approach, their noise terrified my wife and children.

The next morning we started on a second day's tramp in the wilderness, and a painful day it was. The road was rough; the underbrush tore our clothes; trees that had been blown down blocked the way. Faint with hunger, we struggled along, I with my babes on my back, my wife aiding the two other children to climb over the fallen trunks and force themselves through the briers.

I suppose it was about three o'clock in the afternoon when we discerned several persons approaching. We were instantly on the alert, and the advance of a few paces showed me they were Indians. When they saw me, they set up a peculiar howl, turned around, and ran as fast as they could. There were three or four of them, and what they were afraid of I could not imagine, unless they supposed I was the devil, whom they had perhaps heard of as black. My wife thought they were merely running back to collect more of a party and then to come and murder us. I told her they had been numerous enough to do that without help; if they had wanted to. I said that it would be a ridiculous thing if both parties ran away, and that I was going to follow.

We did follow and, as we advanced, we could discern Indians peeping at us from behind the trees and dodging out of sight if they thought we were looking at them. Presently we came upon their wigwams and saw a fine-looking, stately Indian, with his arms folded, waiting for us to approach. He apparently was the chief and saluted us civilly. He soon discovered we were human beings, and spoke to his young men, who were scattered about, and made them come in and give up their foolish fears.

And now curiosity seemed to prevail. Each one wanted to touch the children, who were as shy as partridges after their days in the woods. As they shrank away and uttered little cries of alarm, the Indians would jump back too, as if they thought the children would bite. However, a little while sufficed to make the Indians understand what we were and whither we were going. They fed us bountifully and gave us a comfortable wigwam for our night's rest. The next day we resumed our march, having ascertained from the Indians that we were only about twenty-five miles from the lake [Lake Erie].

One night more was passed in the woods, and the next fore-noon we came out on a wide plain which lies south and west of Sandusky city. The houses of the village were in plain sight. About a mile from the lake I hid my wife and children in the bushes and pushed forward. I was attracted by a house on the left, between which and a small coasting vessel a number of men were passing and repassing. Scarcely had I come within hailing distance when the captain of the schooner cried out, "Hello there, man! you want to work?"

"Yes, sir!" shouted I.

"Come along, come along; I'll give you a shilling an hour. Must get off with this wind."

In a minute I had hold of a bag of corn and followed the gang in emptying it into the hold. I took my place in the line of laborers next to a black man and soon got into conversation with him. "How far is it to Canada?" I asked.

He gave me a peculiar look. "Want to go to Canada? Come along with us, then. Our captain's a fine fellow. We're going to Buffalo."

"Buffalo; how far is that from Canada?"

"Don't you know, man? Just across the river."

I now told him about my wife and children. "I'll speak to the captain," said he.

He did so, and in a moment the captain took me aside. "So you want to go to Buffalo with your family," he said. "Coom, my good fellow, tell us all about it. You're running away, ain't you?"

I saw he was a friend and opened my heart to him.

"How long will it take you to get ready?" he wanted to know.

"Be back here in half an hour, sir."

"Stop," says he. "You go on getting the grain in. When we

get off, I'll lay to over opposite that island and send a boat back. There's a lot of regular nigger-catchers in the town below, and they might suspect if you brought your party out of the bush by daylight."

I worked away with a will. Soon the two or three hundred bushels of corn were aboard, the hatches fastened down, the anchor raised, and the sails hoisted.

I watched the vessel with intense interest as she left her moorings. Away she went before the free breeze. Already she seemed beyond the spot at which the captain agreed to lay to, and still she flew along. My heart sank within me; so near deliverance, and to have my hopes blasted!

The sun had sunk to rest, and the purple and gold of the west were fading away into gray when suddenly the vessel swung round into the wind, the sails flapped, and she stood motionless. A moment more and a boat was lowered from her stern which made for the point at which I stood. I felt that my hour of release had come. On she came, and in ten minutes she rode up handsomely onto the beach.

My black friend and two sailors jumped out, and we started off at once for my wife and children. To my horror, they were gone from the place where I had left them. I supposed they had been found and carried off. The men with me said there was not time to lose, and I would have to go alone.

Just at the point of despair, however, I stumbled on one of the children. My wife, alarmed at my long absence, had given up all for lost. She supposed I had fallen into the hands of the enemy, and when she heard my voice mingled with those of the others she thought my captors were leading me back to make me discover my family. In her terror she had tried to hide herself, and I had hard work to satisfy her. Our long habits of concealment and anxiety had rendered her suspicious of everyone. This, however, was soon over, and the kindness of my companions did much to facilitate the matter.

And now we were off for the boat. It required little time to embark our baggage, one convenience, at least, of having nothing. The men bent their backs with a will and headed steadily for a light hung from the vessel's mast. Three hearty cheers welcomed us as we reached the schooner, and never till my dying day shall I forget the shout of the captain, a Scotsman. "Coom up on deck, mon; you're free now."

Round went the vessel, the wind plunged into her sails, the water seethed and hissed. My happiness rose at last to positive pain. Unnerved by so sudden a change from destitution and danger to such kindness and blessed security, I wept like a child.

The next evening we reached Buffalo, but it was too late to cross the river that night. "You see those trees," said the noble-hearted captain next morning, pointing to a group of trees in the distance. "They grow on free soil, and as soon as your feet touch that, you're a *mon*. I want to see you go and be free. I am poor myself, and have nothing to give you; I only sail the boat for wages; but I'll see you across.

"Here, Green," said he to a ferryman; "what will you take this man and his family over for—he's got no money?"

"Three shillings."

The captain took a dollar out of his pocket and gave it to me. He put his hand on my shoulder and said, "Be a good fellow, won't you?"

I felt streams of emotion running down in electric courses from head to foot. "Yes," said I. "I'll use my freedom well."

He stood waving his hat as we pushed off for the opposite shore. God bless him!

It was the 28th of October, 1830, when my feet first touched the Canada shore. I threw myself on the ground, rolled in the sand, seized handfuls of it and kissed them. I hugged and kissed my wife and children, then—until the first exultant burst of feeling was over—went on dancing around as before. Several of those present shouted with laughter.

"He's some crazy fellow," said one man who was present. "Oh, no, master! don't you know?" I told him. "I'm free."

*   *   *

Josiah Henson found work on a farm owned by a Mr. Hibbard, who sent the oldest boy in the family to school, and the boy taught the father to read. In spite of his later success Henson remained a humble man dedicated to helping his own people and went on several rescue missions into the region where he had once lived. "After I had tasted the blessing of freedom," he said, "I proceeded to take measures to free as many [others] as I could." It was a source of great happiness to him that he was finally able to rescue 118 slaves.

2

Refugees from Czarist Russia

" 'God Bless America,' which I wrote some years ago," said Irving Berlin, "is not alone a song but an expression of my gratitude to the country that inspired it."

The man who was to enrich America with more than a thousand popular songs had been born Israel Baline, the son of a rabbi in Russia when czars ruled the land. All who were not members of the Russian Orthodox Church were persecuted, but none more relentlessly than the Jews. Though little Israel Baline was only four, he never forgot the night in 1892 when the Cossacks, the cavalry troops of the Czar, drove them from their home. The parents with their six children crouched together in a field close by, watching through the night as the town went up in flames. Then and there the rabbi decided he must take his family to America.

Another Russian child, whose family left in 1906 to escape religious persecution, was a girl named Golda Mabovitz. The family settled in Milwaukee, Wisconsin, where they were quite poor, but the girl was a brilliant student in high school and college. At nineteen, she married Morris Myerson, a name later shortened to Meir, and the couple left soon afterward for Palestine. Determined that other Jewish children should be spared experiences such as had scarred her own early years, she threw herself wholeheartedly into the movement to establish an independent homeland for the Jews.

In 1969 Golda Meir became premier of Israel. In several annual polls taken in America of the world's most admired women, her name has ranked high on the list.

Golda was fourteen in 1912 when *The Promised Land* by Mary

13

Antin was published, a book that was to provide native and adopted Americans with a better understanding of one another. To most children brought up in pious Jewish homes, "the promised land" referred to God's promise in the Old Testament that the Hebrew people should one day return to their ancient homeland in Palestine. To Mary, whose father had emigrated from Russia to Boston, the term had come to symbolize the United States. For three years she and other members of her family had waited anxiously for the time when he would have earned enough money to send for them.

At last in 1894 the great day came. As the big ship that carried the Antin family to America "crept nearer and nearer the coveted shore," thirteen-year-old Mary's emotions were in turmoil. The discomforts of the past six weeks in the crowded steerage were forgotten in the realization that her dearest wish would soon be realized.

"On a glorious May morning," she wrote later, "our eyes beheld the promised land."

Probably no refugees of the nineteenth century were more grateful for a chance to come to America than were the Jews who had lived in Russia under the czars. The reasons have been eloquently described in the book that Mary wrote after she grew up.

Mine Eyes Beheld the Promised Land (1894)

BY MARY ANTIN

I do not know when I became old enough to understand. My grandmother told me about it when she put me to bed at night. My playmates told me, when they drew me back into a corner of the gateway to let a policeman pass. Vanko, the little white-haired boy, told me about it, when he ran out of his mother's laundry to throw mud after me when I happened to pass.

Sometimes, waking in the night, I heard my parents whisper it in the dark.

There was no time in my life when I did not hear and see and feel the truth—the reason why our town, Polotzk, was cut off from the rest of Russia. It was the first lesson a little girl in our town had to learn. But for a long while I did not understand. Then there came a time when I knew that Polotzk and Vitebsk and Vilna and some other places were grouped together as the "Pale of Settlement," and within this area the Czar commanded me to stay, with my father and mother and friends, and all other people like us. We must not be found outside the Pale, because we were Jews.

The world was divided into Jews and Gentiles. This knowledge came so gradually that it could not shock me. It trickled into my consciousness drop by drop. By the time I fully understood that I was a prisoner, the shackles had grown familiar to my flesh.

The first time Vanka threw mud at me, I ran home and complained to my mother, who brushed off my dress and said quite resignedly, "How can I help you, my poor child? Vanka is a Gentile. The Gentiles do as they like with us Jews." The next time Vanka spat on me, I wiped my face and thought nothing at all. I accepted ill-usage from the Gentiles as one accepts the weather. The world was made in a certain way, and I had to live in it.

Not quite all the Gentiles were like Vanka. Next door to us lived a Gentile family which was very friendly. There was a girl as big as I, who never called me names, and gave me flowers from her father's garden. And there were the Parphens, of whom my grandfather rented his store. On our festival days they visited our house and brought us presents, carefully choosing such things as Jewish children might accept. My father used to say that if all the Russians were like the Parphens, there would be no trouble between Gentiles and Jews. . . . The Gentiles said that we had killed their God, which was absurd.

Besides, what they accused us of had happened so long ago; the Gentiles themselves said it was long ago. Everybody had been dead for ages who could have had anything to do with it.

Another thing the Gentiles said about us was that we used the blood of murdered Christian children at the Passover festival. Of course that was a wicked lie. It made me sick to think of such a thing. I knew everything that was done for Passover, from the time I was a very little girl. The house was made clean and shining and holy, even in the corners where nobody ever looked. Vessels and dishes that were used all the year round were put away in the garret, and special vessels were brought out for the Passover week. I used to help unpack the new dishes and find my own blue mug. When the fresh curtains were put up, and the white floors were uncovered, and everybody in the house put on new clothes, and I sat down to the feast in my new dress, I felt clean inside and out. . . . The youngest child in the house knew how Passover was kept.

The Passover season, when we celebrated our deliverance from the land of Egypt and felt so glad and thankful, as if it had only just happened, was the time our Gentile neighbors chose to remind us that Russia was another Egypt. That is what I heard people say, and it was true. It was not so bad in Polotzk, within the Pale; but in Russian cities, and even more in the country districts, where Jewish families lived scattered, by special permission of the police, who were always changing their minds about letting them stay, the Gentiles made the Passover a time of horror for the Jews. Somebody would start up that lie about murdering Christian children, and the stupid peasants would get mad about it, and fill themselves with vodka, and set out to kill the Jews. They attacked them with knives and clubs and scythes and axes, killed them or tortured them, and burned their houses.

This was called a "pogrom." Jews who escaped the pogroms came to Polotzk with wounds on them, and horrible, horrible stories. To hear them made one sob and choke with pain. I never was in an actual pogrom, but there were times when it threatened us even in Polotzk.

I remember a time when I thought a pogrom had broken out in our street. It was some Christian holiday, and we had been warned by the police to keep indoors. Gates were locked; shutters were barred. Fearful yet curious, we looked through the cracks in the shutters. We saw a procession of peasants and townspeople, led by a number of priests, and there were soldiers and police. I asked the nurse what the soldiers were for. Thoughtlessly she answered me, "In case of a pogrom." I wonder that I did not die of fear.

The Gentiles used to wonder at us because we cared so much about religious things—about food, and Sabbath, and teaching the children Hebrew. They were angry with us for our obstinacy, as they called it, and mocked us and ridiculed the most sacred things. There were wise Gentiles who understood. These were educated people, like Fedora Pavlovna, who made friends with their Jewish neighbors. They were always respectful, and openly admired some of our ways. But most of the Gentiles were ignorant and distrustful and spiteful. They would not believe that there was any good in our religion, and of course we dared not teach them, because we should be accused of trying to convert them, and that would be the end of us. Oh, if they could only understand!

In your father's parlor hung a large colored portrait of Alexander III. The Czar was a cruel tyrant. Oh, it was whispered when doors were locked and shutters tightly barred at night, yet his portrait was seen in a place of honor in your father's house. You knew why. It looked well when police or government officers came on business.

You went out to play one morning and saw a little knot of people gathered around a lamppost. There was a notice on it —a new order from the chief of police. You pushed into the crowd and stared at the placard. A woman with a ragged shawl looked down upon you and said, with a bitter kind of smile,

"Rejoice, rejoice, little girl! The chief of police bids you rejoice. There shall be a pretty flag flying from every housetop today, because it is the Czar's birthday, and we must celebrate. Come and watch the poor people pawn their samovars and candlesticks, to raise money for a pretty flag. It is a holiday, little girl. Rejoice!"

You know the woman is mocking. You are familiar with the quality of that smile. You know it is no joke. The flag must show from every house, or the owner will be dragged to the police.

It was bewildering to hear how many kinds of duties and taxes we owed the Czar. We paid taxes on our houses and taxes on the rents from the houses, taxes on our business, taxes on our profits. I am not sure whether there were taxes on our losses. The town collected taxes, and the county, and the central government; and the chief of police we had always with us. Business really did not pay when the price of goods was so swollen by taxes that the people could not buy. The only way to make business pay was to cheat—cheat the government of part of the duties. But playing tricks on the Czar was dangerous, with so many spies watching his interests. The constant risk, the worry, the dread of a police raid in the night, and the ruinous fines, in case of detection, left very little margin of profit or comfort to the dealer in contraband goods.

"But what can one do?" the people said, with the shrug of the shoulders that expressed the helplessness of the Pale. "What can one do? One must live."

It was not easy to live, with such bitter competition as the congestion of population made inevitable. There were ten times as many stores as there should have been, ten times as many tailors, cobblers, barbers, tinsmiths. A Gentile, if he failed in Polotzk, could go elsewhere, where there was less competition. A Jew could make the circle of the Pale, only to find the same conditions as at home. Outside the Pale he could only go to certain designated localities, on payment of prohibitive fees, augmented by a constant stream of bribes; and even then he lived at the mercy of the local chief of police.

The Gentiles had their excuse for their malice. They said our merchants and money-lenders preyed upon them, and our shopkeepers gave false measure. People who want to defend the Jews ought never to deny this. Yes, I say, we cheated the Gentiles whenever we dared, because it was the only thing to do. Remember how the Czar was always sending us commands —you shall not do this and you shall not do that, until there was little left that we might honestly do, except pay tribute and die. There he had us cooped up, thousands of us where only hundreds could live, and every means of living taxed to the utmost.

A favorite complaint against us was that we were greedy for gold. Greedy for profits we were, eager for bargains, for savings, intent on squeezing the utmost out of every business transaction. But why? Did not the Gentiles know the reason? Did they not know what price we had to pay for the air we breathed? If a Jew and a Gentile kept store side by side, the Gentile could content himself with smaller profits. He did not have to buy permission to travel in the interests of his business. He was saved the expense of hushing inciters of pogroms. Police favor was retailed at a lower price to him than to the Jew. Is it any wonder that we hoarded our pennies?

As I look back today I see, within the wall raised around my birthplace by the vigilance of the police, another wall, higher, thicker, more impenetrable. This is the wall which the Czar with all his minions could not shake. This wall within the wall is the religious integrity of the Jews, a fortress erected by the prisoners of the Pale in defiance of their jailers. Harassed on every side, thwarted in every normal effort, pent up within narrow limits, the Russian Jew fell back upon the only thing that never failed him—his hereditary faith in God.

What did it matter to us, on a Sabbath or festival, when our life was centered in the synagogue, what czar sat on the throne, what evil counselors whispered in his ear? They were concerned with revenues and policies and ephemeral trifles of all sorts, while we were intent on renewing our ancient covenant with God, to the end that His promise to the world should be fulfilled.

* * *

In the tenement district of Boston where Mr. Antin took his family to live, they were quite poor, but education was free. "This comprised his chief hope for us children," Mary was to write later, "the essence of American opportunity, the treasure that no thief could touch, not even misfortune or poverty. It was the one thing he was able to promise us; surer, safer than bread or butter."

In the Boston public schools, Mary was a brilliant student. Leading citizens were her friends, and she was encouraged to continue her education. At the age of twenty she married Amadeus Grabau, a professor at Columbia University, and ten years later published *The Promised Land.*

3

An Escapee from Armenia

"The reason this book was written was that there are some things I wanted to say about America . . . and thought that it was time somebody did."

It was with these words that George M. Mardikian, well-known civic leader and restaurateur, opened his volume of reminiscences, *Song of America.* He was less concerned by the fact that his adopted country had not yet lived up to all of the ideals of its founders than by his conviction that so many of the ideals had indeed been realized. "Yes, I want to shout the glories of America," he said. "I've seen the other side."

To a young man who arrived from war-torn Armenia in the early 1920s, the United States was a haven to be desired above all others. Even before that part of the ancient land now known as Armenia was absorbed by the Soviet Union, it had long been a battleground for the armies of opposing nations. During World War I when George Mardikian was growing up, Turkey was in control and fighting against Russia. Fearing that the Armenians might aid the enemy, hundreds of thousands of helpless people were driven into the Arabian desert to die of heat and starvation.

Most of those who survived the ordeal had Near East Relief to thank. This organization, made up of American and Canadian physicians, nurses, teachers, mechanics, engineers, and industrial experts, employed thousands of native workers to aid in the enormous task of relieving the suffering of a devastated country. In one orphanage alone—the largest in the world—more than 21,000 children were cared for. Here "Uncle America," as they often referred to the relief

workers, provided them with food and clothing and real beds to sleep
on. Girls learned to sew and cook. Boys were taught to farm or were
instructed in some trade that would enable them to make a living
later on. Near East Relief held out the only hope for thousands of
homeless Armenians during that difficult time.

The Armenian—and the American—Way (1922)

BY GEORGE M. MARDIKIAN

Armenia today is scarcely as large as Delaware and Maryland—just another forgotten "republic" in the grim Soviet Union. But another Armenia lives in the hearts of people scattered over the world: the Armenia that once stretched from
the Black Sea to the Caspian; the Armenia that for 3,000 years
fought off Assyrians, Romans, Mongols, Persians, Turks, Russians; the Armenia that was a great Christian nation long
before the gospels reached Western Europe. This is *my* Armenia.

In 1895, after my parents were married, Sultan Abdul Ha-
mid II of Turkey set out to massacre every Armenian from the
Caucasus to the Dardanelles. . . . My parents went to Istanbul,
the Turkish capital, where Armenians were safer because of
the foreign embassies, and then to Tiflis in the Russian Caucasus. There my sister Baidzar, my brother Arshag, and I were
born.

When I was five the Young Turks deposed the Sultan and the
Armenians hailed this hopefully as "the liberation." Our family
moved to Scutari, on a beautiful hillside within sight of the

domes and minarets of Istanbul. But our good times here stopped after Turkey entered World War I on Germany's side, against Great Britain and Russia and, later, against the United States. The big guns of the British fleet grumbled in the distance every night, and with the sound of guns our heritage haunted us once more—a bitter heritage of homeless wandering, wars, persecution, and murder. We drew our curtains and darkened our rooms and locked our doors. When I had to go out at night to buy food, I walked in the middle of the street, as my father told me. We had heard there were Turkish massacres to the south, and I carried sharp stones in my pocket to fight back with in case I was attacked.

In April, 1915, the Turks said that the Armenians were aiding the Allies. With this as their excuse they set out once more to exterminate my race. They "deported" thousands of Armenians, driving them from their homes and leading them into the deserts to die there like abandoned dogs.

One night toward the end of that month there was a terrible pounding on our door, and Turkish officers came in and took my father. He was one of hundreds they seized in Scutari and Istanbul that night—the elite of Armenian manhood. I never saw my father again. The month after that my mother's mother and her whole family were driven from their home. A fire of hatred burned in my breast. To take revenge for the wrongs done to my people and to make my mother proud of a warrior son, I ran away to fight against the Turks, as my ancestors before me had done for 3,000 years.

I was fifteen, and there were hundreds of others my age and younger, and the ragged legion we marched and starved and fought with helped to win Armenia's first independence in seven centuries. What a wonderful achievement that was! But it was only one of the many breathtaking changes: the mighty Russian Czar overthrown, Russia torn by the Bolshevik revolt, and Turkey, her sovereignty lost, in the hands of Allied occupation forces. Our world had been shaken apart.

The Caucasus country was in chaos. Although I tried to get word through to my mother that I was alive and safe, she never heard from me. Nor could I take a trip back home. How could I leave for one day, let alone a week or a month, our baby republic that needed every bit of help she could get? Unification and the training of her youth were essential. I pitched in at Kars to organize Armenian boy-scout troops.

One day in summer, 1920, I called on Captain Eddie Fox, district director of Near East Relief at Kars. On his office wall hung the picture of a strange-looking man. In Armenia, grown men wore full beards and big mustaches, but this man had a little stubby beard and no mustache at all. When we began talking about my country, Captain Fox pointed to the picture and said, "What Armenia needs is a man like him—an Abe Lincoln."

This was the first picture of Abraham Lincoln that I had ever seen. As I studied it and saw what was in his face, my heart was filled with awe and reverence. He would have understood my country and her heartbreaking struggle for freedom. The boys who might have become her Lincolns seldom survived until manhood.

Then I met another American, another Near East Relief official, George D. White. He opened his warehouse door and said, "If there is anything here you need for your scouts, take it. It's yours."

He found footballs and baseballs for Armenian boys who wouldn't have known what to do with them, because they had never learned how to play football or baseball, or any other game.

Before we ever had a chance to use those footballs and baseballs, there came another war, with the Turks in front of us and the Russians behind us. It destroyed the last hopes of the Armenian nation and left it a Soviet vassal.

The Turks captured 200 of us and threw us into a foul-smelling sauerkraut factory in Kars. We were packed in so

tightly we couldn't lie down at night. By day we chopped ice
on the Kars River, and every night some of us died from cold
and exposure. When I was taken prisoner, I was a husky ath-
lete; within three weeks I weighed 110 pounds. Only my hands
and feet looked plump; they were puffy and swollen because
they had been frozen.

There comes a time when you know you are finished. One
morning my spirit broke and I gave up in despair. I had a
desperate desire to send a last message to my mother. My only
chance was to bribe the Turkish guard.

I went up to him on the way to the river ice pack.

"Let me stand by the road until the Near East Relief official
drives by and I will get you some condensed milk," I said. To
sweets-loving Turks, condensed milk was manna itself.

He was going to kill me eventually, anyway; what did he
have to lose? He growled and told me to hurry.

Too weak to stand, I lay shivering in the snow by the river
bridge until a Near East Relief car came past. Luckily for me,
Mr. White and his wife, Elsie, were in it. I was so thin he could
hardly believe me when I told him I was Scoutmaster Mardikian. Tears came to Mrs. White's eyes. She wrapped me in
her fur coat. They promised to rescue me.

"It's too late," I said. "I'm going to die. All I want is to send
word to my mother, to say goodbye." I gave them my mother's
name and address. "Now, if you really wish to help me—this
minute—give me two cans of condensed milk."

Clutching the cans, I turned and hobbled away hurriedly so
that the Americans wouldn't see my tears.

That night a guard called my name. My time, I thought, had
come. But instead of taking me behind the Armenian church
where the executions took place, he led me to the office of the
Turkish commandant. Mr. White was standing there.

"Mardikian," the commandant roared, "why didn't you tell
us you are an American?"

I was dumfounded; then I saw Mr. White wink. "I'm sorry, sir," I said. "You didn't give me a chance."

"Just being an American doesn't release you, but we're going to send you to the hospital. Thank your friend here for that." And he jerked his head at Mr. White.

After three weeks in the American-supervised hospital, I worked in Near East Relief warehouses. When my strength returned, Mr. White slipped me and another prisoner canned food, shoes, and blankets, and one night we ran away. We hid in caves by day and traveled by night. It took ten nights to make our way through the snow to Erevan, on the Transcaucasus border.

There Dr. Clarence Usher, an American physician turned missionary, defied Bolshevik threats of death to anyone harboring a prisoner or "an enemy of the state" and gave us shelter. I stayed with him in the American Mission House until my frozen feet were healed. Then, disguised as an American in a Near East Relief uniform, I went by train to Alexandropol. There I was made chief guard for the barracks in which 21,000 Armenian orphans were housed and fed.

Those who lived in more fortunate countries had forgotten that people in our section of the world had no food—all but the Americans who came to our rescue. In the summer of 1921 a group of their distinguished leaders—senators, representatives, and others—came to Armenia to visit our orphanages and survey the relief situation. We all marched to the railroad station to greet them, and later, on the field, we raised the American flag. The orphans, parading back and forth, spelled out, "Thank you, America and N.E.R. [Near East Relief]."

Dr. John Voris, who was in charge of the education department of Near East Relief, stood on a platform beneath the flagstaff and the American flag and gave a talk. None of us would ever forget it, for it filled us with faith.

"Do not give up hope," he said. "America knows about you, and America will see to it that you are fed and clothed and kept warm."

Men like Mr. White, Captain Fox, and now Dr. Voris made me lie awake in my bunk at night, dreaming about the bright country across the Atlantic. I pictured life as it must be in that wonderful land—the happiness, the freedom, the opportunity to earn money to send back to my mother, much more money than I could ever hope to make in Istanbul.

Later I learned that Mother and my little sister Arlene were safe in Scutari. So, disguised again as an American relief worker, I rode a supply train north to Tiflis. Somehow, N.E.R. supervisors smuggled me into the wax-sealed freight car of a train bound for Batumi. There, with a gang of relief workers, I walked aboard a French supply ship. Her sailing whistle blew. My comrades hurried ashore. But I stayed below and hid among the crates and bales of the cargo. The sailors pulled in the gangplank and cast off, and the ship steered west—for Istanbul.

Everyone had told my mother that I must be dead. But she kept insisting that it was not true. Beside the front door in most Near Eastern homes, at about shoulder height, is a small sheltered niche for the burning of the *gantegh*, which is a little oil lamp. When you see one of these burning at night, you know that a loved one is far away. It is a sign that those in the house are thinking of him and anxiously awaiting his return.

Every night since the night so long ago when I had run away, my mother had lighted the *gantegh*, as a symbol of her hope that I would come back safe. It was dark when I finally climbed the hill to home and stood beside the lighted lamp—a little choked because I knew who had kept it lighted. Arlene came flying to the door. She cried my name and threw her arms around me.

Over her shoulder, through my tears, I saw my dear mother, drying her hands on her apron and saying softly, "I knew this day would come. I knew God would be kind—" Then her arms were around me. Neither she nor I could speak.

After supper we sat around the table and laughed and cried and talked far into the night. We talked about my brother

Arshag and my sister Baidzar, who had gone together to America where Baidzar had married a successful tailor named Aram. Their letters told how happy they were and how they were living for the day when we could join them. Arshag said he was going to send me money to help me go to America.

Then I told Mother about the Americans I had met—about how kind they were. She pressed my hand. "I want you to go —soon, my son," she said. She smiled down at Arlene. "We shall follow and all be together again in the New World."

Soon a letter from Arshag arrived, telling me to hurry to America, to where he was in San Francisco, California. With the letter came some money. That first week in June, 1922, I managed to book passage on the Greek steamer *Meghali Ellas*, which means "mighty Greece." Its destination was New York —and the land of my dreams.

My mother polished the brass *gantegh*, so she could burn it beside the door again for me. Neither of us said anything about it, but I knew we were both praying that it would burn, not until I came home again, but until she shut the door of that house forever and started the long journey to me and her other loved ones in America. She stood straight and tall in the doorway that morning, waving goodbye. Her shining face was filled with love.

"Until we meet again, my son!" she called.

My little sister Arlene buried her face in Mother's skirts. I couldn't say a word. I waved back and hurried down the street, down the hill, for the last time.

An hour after the ship sailed, Turkish *jandarmas*—armed police—pounded on my mother's door. When she answered, they pushed her aside. "We have come for your son," said their leader. "The one who has been masquerading as a Near East Relief worker."

My mother smiled. "Search the house if you wish."

Something in her voice—amusement, or pride, or contempt, or all three—made them hesitate.

"You are too late," she said. "He has escaped you forever."

They thought I had died, that that was what my mother had meant. It was the only way I could escape them that they could think of.

"No," my mother said, still smiling, "he has not died. He has just begun to live."

They ransacked the house from attic to cellar. Then, grumbling, they went away.

You must picture me at the age of eighteen. A snapshot I remember shows me standing self-consciously against the steerage rail of the *Meghali Ellas*, awkward in my new store-made suit and the round felt hat perched squarely on top of my head. As the Old World vanished over the horizon, I thought of all that I had left behind—the bitter days, the brave dead, the broken dreams. Twelve days later we saw in the soft morning glow the outlines of New York's skyscrapers and that beautiful lady, the Statue of Liberty, with her torch and crown. We stood there speechless. Some were weeping. We were the tired, the poor, the homeless ones she asked for.

On Ellis Island we were handed big white towels and bars of soap and escorted to the showers. The attendant showed us how to work the hot and cold water taps.

"How much hot water can we have?" I asked.

He grinned. "All you want!"

I didn't believe him. But minutes went by and the hot water never stopped. I scrubbed harder and harder. I washed away the Old World. When I dried myself with the heavy towel I felt like a new human being, taller, stronger, prouder. Ever since, I have celebrated the day of that shower—July 24—as my birthday.

Ladies from the Travelers' Aid found me and handed me a railroad ticket and $20 from Arshag, in California. A man tied to my lapel a tag stating my name and destination. The next thing I knew I was on a train and New York was behind me. The train trip across the continent took eight days, and I

thought of the pioneers who had crossed the continent looking
for this promised land. They had been immigrants like me. Did
I have their strength and courage? Were there still opportunities left? A thousand hopes, doubts, fears, raced through my
head. . . . Then I was in San Francisco, with Baidzar's and
Arshag's arms around me.

In time George Mardikian's mother and younger sister realized
their dream to join the family in America. In the meantime much
had happened to George. His first job was washing dishes at Coffee
Dan's, an all-night lunch stand he later was able to buy. In 1932, three
years after he became a naturalized citizen, he founded Omar
Khayyam's, soon to become a famous restaurant in San Francisco. As
a civic leader in his adopted city, he served on the executive boards
of the Boys' Clubs and the Boy Scouts, and during World War II he
was an enthusiastic seller of defense bonds. The hard, cold winter of
1946–47 found him in Europe, visiting the Displaced Persons' camps
set up by the United Nations Relief and Rehabilitation Administra-
tion. But UNRRA was about to go out of existence, and he was gravely
disturbed about what would happen to more than 4,500 Armenians
who had found temporary refuge in the camps. He then founded and
became the first president of the American Committee to Aid Homeless Armenians, and by the end of 1947 headquarters had been established in Stuttgart, Germany. His story continues.

A wonderful thing had developed. Our Armenian Americans were willing to give more than their money. They were
ready, as American citizens, to sponsor individual DPs—to find
them homes and jobs, guarantee their livelihood until they
were self-supporting.

I was in Fresno, California, when the first contingent of
Armenian DPs arrived. There was one frail little woman, Mrs.
Mariam Mateosian, 99 years old—the oldest immigrant ever to
enter the United States. When we helped her from the train
in Fresno, the tears were streaming down her cheeks.

"Why are you crying, mother?" Arshag asked.

"I am crying for happiness, my son," she said. "I have cried so much in sorrow that I have tears left only for happiness."

Mother Mateosian had survived two Turkish massacres, the Soviet conquest of Armenia, the German invasion of the Crimea, and two Nazi concentration camps. When she died a few years later at the age of 104 she was a revered citizen of Fresno.

Within the next few years some 4,000 displaced Armenians were settled in the United States, many of them in my own beloved California, where I could watch their progress with pride. They proved worthy followers of the older Armenians who had transformed the San Joaquin Valley into one of the garden spots of the world.

Men who were once doctors and lawyers were now picking grapes and cotton, plowing fields and harvesting wheat. Musicians pumped gas and artists became sign painters' assistants. I watched them in the schoolrooms studying English when their day's work was done. They were all happy, grateful people, living for the day when they would be American citizens.

More than 90 percent of those formerly homeless wanderers have already paid back every penny that was spent to bring them here. They knew that the money was needed for others who were less fortunate. That is the Armenian—and the American—way. . . .

One morning I found a letter on White House stationery in my mail. It was an invitation to a small stag dinner, signed by Dwight D. Eisenhower. There were just seventeen guests, and we dined on terrapin soup and steaks. Later we sat with the President, discussing world affairs.

For a long time the President listened. Then he said; "My friends, the biggest, most powerful weapon that America has is not the atomic bomb or the H-bomb or even the superb fighting ability of its officers and men. It is the moral and spiritual strength of millions of Americans. Nothing can ever conquer that strength. Remember that, gentlemen, because that is the weapon that America's enemies really fear."

I knew what he meant! O Lord, I believe it with all my heart!

When we said good night and walked down the White House steps, I refused offers of a ride back to my hotel. I wanted to walk. There were things I wanted to think about.

Where else could it have happened? Where else could an immigrant boy, tired and dispirited, find such opportunities to make his dreams come true? Where else could a man, humble and grateful, find the freedom to share his blessings with so many?

4

Famous Exiles from Italy

One of the best-known exiles ever to seek refuge in America was Giuseppe Garibaldi, leader in the long and bitter struggle to free Italy from foreign rule. In 1850 when his ship docked in New York, his arrival was hailed by the New York *Tribune* because of "his chivalrous character and his services in behalf of liberty."

During the next few years Garibaldi worked as a candlemaker on Staten Island and became a naturalized American citizen, but his native land still needed him. He returned to Italy to fight again and was there during the American Civil War. President Lincoln offered him a commission as a major general in the Union Army, but by then Garibaldi had been wounded in battle. He agreed that, as soon as he recovered, he would welcome an opportunity "to serve the great American public . . . dear to him." His wounds, though, were more serious than he had realized, and before he could fulfill his promise the Civil War came to an end.

Meanwhile in 1852 an artist who had been imprisoned in Italy for his political beliefs had sought sanctuary in Washington, D.C. Here Constantino Brumidi began the work that was to occupy him during the last thirty years of his life, covering the walls of the nation's capitol with the frescoes that may be seen there today. Some of the paintings were of allegorical scenes; others depicted famous scenes from American history. On the fresco showing the triumph of General Washington at Yorktown, the new naturalized American proudly signed his name: *"C. Brumidi, Artist, Citizen of the U.S."* That was how he wanted to be remembered.

"My one ambition and my daily prayer," he said, "is that I may live

33

long enough to make beautiful the capitol of the one country in the world in which there is liberty."

Both Brumidi and Garibaldi lived to see their native land become a free, united nation. But though a picturesque country, Italy was still a very poor one. It suffered heavy losses during World War I, and the unrest and hard times opened the way in 1922 for a dictator, Benito Mussolini, to gain control of the government. Mussolini, founder of the Fascist Party, tried to appeal to the Italians by reminding them of Italy's ancient glory, but under fascism they were deprived of fundamental human rights. Conditions worsened after he formed an alliance with the German dictator, Adolf Hitler, in 1936.

The situation that decided some of the country's intellectuals to leave the country has been vividly described by the wife of one of the world's great scientists, Enrico Fermi. The following selection is from her book *Atoms in the Family.*

Columbus of the Atomic Age (1938)

BY LAURA FERMI

A telephone that rings early in the morning has a peculiar quality. It is sudden and startling, shrill and peremptory. You are shocked out of your last dreams, you are forced out of your bed. So, early on the morning of November 10, 1938, I found myself answering the telephone in the hall of our apartment in Rome.

"Is this Professor Fermi's residence?" asked the operator's voice.

"Yes, indeed."

"I wish to inform you that this evening at six Professor Fermi will be called on the telephone from Stockholm."

My drowsiness vanished at once. A call from Stockholm! I could guess the implications of a call from Stockholm! My slippers banged louder and louder with noisy excitement as I ran on the terrazzo floors from the hall back into our bedroom.

"Wake up, Enrico! This evening you'll be called on the telephone from Stockholm!"

Calm, but immediately alert, my husband propped himself up on his elbow and replied, "It must mean the Nobel Prize."

"Of course it does!"

"So the possibilities that were hinted to me have become true, and it was right to make our plans as we did."

At this reference to our plans my excitement subsided.

According to our plans we would leave Italy for good early next year. But if Enrico were to be awarded the Nobel Prize, we would leave sooner, in less than a month, go to Stockholm, and then directly on to the United States without coming back home at all. Our plans were the most sensible under the circumstances. Yet the thought of leaving Rome gave me pain. I was born there. I had always lived there. My relatives, my friends, were there. I belonged in Rome. My roots were so firm, they reached so deeply into the rich soil of memories, habits, and affections, that I felt I would not be easily transplanted.

In past years Enrico had often suggested that we should leave Italy to escape fascism, and move to the United States; each time I had raised objections. Fascism so far had been a mild dictatorship and had not interfered with the private life of people who, like us, did not put their criticism and disapproval into action. The great majority of Italians were politically inactive; they let themselves be dragged downstream by the strong current and did not struggle against it. Despite fascism, life in Rome had been pleasant for us, and we had stayed.

Circumstances were different in 1938. It was almost unbelievable that fascism, under the Italian *Duce* Mussolini, had entered into an alliance with Nazi Germany under Hitler. The Germans had been the traditional foes of Italians, since the

First World War. The newly risen Führer of Germany was held
to be a none-too-intelligent imitator of the *Duce,* a puppet
obediently waiting for directives from the fascist master. The
puppet had taken some initiative of his own. In March, 1935,
he had denounced the Versailles Treaty and declared that
Germany would rearm. In March, 1936, his troops occupied
the demilitarized Rhineland. Though Mussolini dreaded a
strong Germany, by then he was on bad terms with France and
England, and the following July Germany and Italy found
themselves together, unofficially fighting on the same side in
the Spanish war.

From then on there was avowed friendship between the two
dictators, and the Rome-Berlin Axis came into being on October 23, 1936. The *Duce* still lived in the delusion that he was
the boss and that he had Hitler well in hand. Abruptly, his
delusion was shattered by the *Anschluss.* On March 12, 1938,
Hitler occupied Austria without consulting or even informing
Mussolini. He knew only too well that his friend would object
violently: for years Mussolini had loudly played his self-
assumed role of Austria's protector. When the *Anschluss* was
announced, papers and news broadcasts took no stand for
hours. Mussolini had not decided yet whether to be publicly
outraged, as he certainly was in private, and admit he had been
fooled or to give his wholehearted approval and submit to the
fait accompli. Soon the press burst out in praises for the Führer's statesmanship, for the union of two nations that always
had wanted to be one. Mussolini had saved his face. But Italy
had become Germany's slave.

The consequences of this enslavement were felt only too
soon: in the summer of the same year, 1938, Mussolini
launched an anti-Semitic campaign, for which there were no
reasons, no excuses. No real anti-Semitism existed in Italy, and
Mussolini himself had so declared on several occasions. True,
a few careers were more difficult for Jews to enter. True, my
father had been suddenly and unaccountably dismissed from

active service in the Navy and placed in the reserve. Still these were scattered incidents. There were no Jews and "Aryans," only Italians. Jews represented one per thousand of the population and were destined to decrease in number through the ever-increasing rate of mixed marriages.

Shortly before our departure I overheard a man in working clothes ask another in Rome; "Now they are sending away the Jews. But who are the Jews?"

There were no Jews in southern Italy or in Sicily. From the *podestà*, the mayor, of a remote village in Sicily Mussolini was said to have received a telegram. "Re: Anti-Semitic campaign. Text: Send specimen so we can start campaign." No indications of a racial policy were in sight at the beginning of July, when I left Rome with the children to spend the summer in the Alps. We had rented a house in San Martino, and I was happy to relax, to watch the children become healthily tanned in the rich sunshine. I forgot fascism, Nazism, and the troubles of Europe. I read no newspaper, listened to no broadcast.

August brought Enrico to San Martino. He appeared to be preoccupied, and I asked him why.

"Haven't you noticed what's going on?"

On July 14, he explained, the *Manifesto della Razza* had been published, a document which tried to hide its contradictions in redundancy of phraseology. Separate human races exist, the manifesto stated. The Italian population is of Aryan race. Because there has not been a recent influx of masses into Italy, it can be asserted that by now there exists a pure Italian race. The most blatant contradiction of the manifesto concerned the Jews. It seemed as though the compilers of the manifesto found it expedient to make a distinction between Jews and Semites. The paragraph on the Jews read as follows:

"JEWS DO NOT BELONG TO THE ITALIAN RACE—Of the Semites who through the centuries landed on the sacred soil of our country, nothing is left. Also the Arab occupation of Sicily has left nothing except a memory in a few names; anyhow, the process of assimilation was always very rapid in Italy. The Jews represent the only population that could never be assimilated in Italy, because they are constituted of non-European racial elements, absolutely different from the elements that gave origin to the Italians."

To the honor of Italians, it must be said that Mussolini had great difficulty finding university professors willing to sign this manifesto. Not a single anthropologist put his signature to the document.

The racial campaign, so brilliantly launched, acquired momentum at an amazingly fast pace. The first anti-Semitic laws were passed early in September, 1938. We at once decided to leave Italy as soon as possible. Enrico and our children were Catholics, and we could have stayed. But there is a limit to what one is willing to tolerate.

Afraid that our passports might be withdrawn if our true intentions were known, we were faced with the problem of organizing our departure in secrecy. Foreign mail was likely to be censored. Enrico wrote four letters to four American universities, in which he stated that his reasons for not accepting their previous offers had ceased to be. He dared write nothing more specific.

We were still in the Alps and four letters, all in the same handwriting, all going to America, if mailed at the same village, could not fail to arouse suspicion. We took advantage of a car trip and mailed Enrico's letters at four towns miles apart.

Enrico had several offers of positions in America. He accepted that of Columbia University. To Italian officials he declared that he was embarking on a six-month visit to New York.

Then an unexpected complication came to modify our plans. In October, at a physics meeting in Copenhagen, Enrico was confidentially informed that his name had been mentioned with others for the Nobel Prize, and he was asked whether he would rather have his name temporarily withdrawn in view of the political situation and of the Italian monetary restrictions.

Under normal circumstances any information concerning the Nobel Prize is strictly secret, but it was thought permissible to break the rules in this case.

To prospective emigrants who would be allowed to take only fifty dollars apiece when leaving Italy for good, the Nobel Prize would be a godsend. However, the existing monetary laws required Italian citizens to convert any foreign holdings into lire and bring them into Italy. Hence our decision to go to Stockholm and from there directly to the United States, if Enrico were to be awarded the Nobel Prize.

Then came November 10 and the early telephone call.

"Let's celebrate," I said. "Don't go to work today. Let's go out together."

Thus a while later we were out in the streets of Rome and on a buying spree. We bought a new watch for each of us. I was proud of mine, but at the same time I felt remorse. "We have spent so much money," I said. "Now, if that telephone call does not mean the Nobel Prize. . . . What are we going to do?"

"The probability that the call means the Nobel Prize, or part of it, in case it should be awarded to two physicists together, is at least 90 percent. Even if it does not, we can afford a watch. Besides, we should take along a few objects when we leave. I wouldn't try to purchase diamonds because records of their sales are kept, and we don't care to have our names on records of that kind. A watch is the thing to buy. Inconspicuous and useful."

For the second time since the morning I was reminded that these were my last days in Rome. But I was determined to be of good cheer and to chase away the nostalgia that came over me at the familiar sight of the Roman streets; of the old, faded buildings that had preserved their full charm; of the clumps of ancient trees that everywhere interrupted the monotony of the streets, rising above a discolored wall or behind an iron fence, silent and monumental witnesses to human restlessness;

of the numberless fountains of Rome, which indulged in the
opulence of their water, shot it toward the sky, and let it come
back in cascades of diamondlike droplets, in rainbow patterns.
I was going to enjoy these sights and give thanks to God for
thirty years of life in Rome.

At home the afternoon hours stretched out forever. Would
six o'clock never come? I asked the mute telephone every
time I passed it in the hall.

At a quarter of six Enrico and I sat down to wait in the living
room. When the telephone rang, I ran into the hall.

"I'll take it," I said.

It was not Stockholm but our friend, Ginestra Amaldi.
"Haven't you had that call yet?" she asked. "Some of the people from the lab are here. Call us as soon as you have talked
to Stockholm."

I sat down again. "It is six o'clock," said Enrico. "I'll turn on
the radio, and we'll listen to the news while we wait."

We had become accustomed to being often upset by radio
announcements during the last months. This time it was worse
than ever.

Hard, emphatic, pitiless, the commentator's voice read the
second set of racial laws. The laws issued that day limited the
activities and the civil status of the Jews. Their children were
excluded from public schools. Jewish teachers were dismissed.
Jewish lawyers, physicians, and other professionals could practice for Jewish clients only. Many Jewish firms were dissolved.
"Aryan" servants were not allowed to work for Jews or to live
in their homes. Jews were to be deprived of full citizenship
rights, and their passports would be withdrawn. All my relatives and several of our friends would be affected, would have
to reorganize their lives somehow. Would they succeed? . . .

The telephone call from Stockholm eventually came
through, and it did mean the Nobel Prize. It had been divided
between Enrico and another physicist, as we thought it might.
The secretary of the Swedish Academy of Sciences read the

citation over the telephone. I did not know whether to be happy or sad, whether to heed the telephone or the radio.

A few minutes later the doorbell rang. Ginestra, her soft smile full of sweetness, headed a line of a dozen people. Our friends had come to congratulate Enrico.

"We are going to stay for dinner," Ginestra brazenly said, with no question or hesitation in her voice as she walked into the hall. Thus the house, so quiet and subdued a minute earlier, broke out in merry confusion. The maid was instructed to set a long table, the cook consulted on how to turn our family supper into a banquet; ready-cooked food was sent for; wine was made ready for the celebration. Infected with everybody's excitement, our little boy, Giulio, tried to climb men's legs, to get our friends' attention, while his big sister, Nella, vainly strove to teach him good manners.

Our celebration of the Nobel Prize was Ginestra's scheme, and a successful one, so that we should not brood over the new racial laws.

On December 6, 1938, we left Rome, and the journey to Stockholm was as comfortable as a train journey can be with two weary children who were soon to be eight and three years old respectively. During the past month we had been under constant fear, common to all who plan to leave a country under difficult political circumstances, that we might not succeed in carrying out our projects. Something, we thought, might come up between our plans and their completion, a specific act of the government against us, a new law, the sudden closing of international frontiers, or the outbreak of war.

Enrico had never admitted he was worried. Yet he seemed relieved when the Italian guards at the Brenner Pass had examined our passports and returned them to us with no comments.

Then it was a German guard's turn to inspect our passports. He was standing in the corridor outside the door of our bed-

room, stiff and official, a personification of our past and present
anxieties. He turned our passports in his hands searchingly and
appeared unsatisfied. Enrico rose from his seat and stood in the
corridor, waiting, his thin lips so tightly pressed together that
they had disappeared inside his mouth. The moment unfolded
with unbearable slowness. Nella, always sensitive to our
moods, became restless. Why, she wanted to know, was the
gentleman taking so long with our passports? Why did he turn
all the pages over and over again? Did I think something was
wrong? Would the man send us back to Rome and to Mussolini?

"Be quiet, Nella. Everything is all right!"

Everything had to be all right. Once I had accepted the
decision to leave Italy, I felt as if I had always wanted to leave;
as if all my yearnings and expectations had built up over the
years in one direction: America; as if failure to continue our
journey now would offset a lifelong dream.

Enrico spoke to the guard in German: Was anything the
matter? Had we obtained a visa from the German Konsulat?
the guard asked. He did not seem to find it in our passports.
When Enrico turned the pages and pointed out the visa, the
stiffness vanished from his muscles, his thin lips were visible
once more. The German guard saluted and smiled. Germans
and Italians were good friends, were they not?

"Now, Nella, you can go back to sleep. Nothing was wrong.
Now climb into the berth with Giulio and take care not to wake
him up. Soon the train will start moving and will rock you."

Luckily I had no premonition of all that lay ahead. The war
was to come. The German occupation of Italy was to result in
tragedy for most Italians and in a more urgent, immediate
tragedy for the Italian Jews. Some fled to hide in the Italian
mountains, and some crossed the Alps on foot, into the relative
security of Swiss concentration camps. They were guided by
smugglers who knew the unguarded passes, who helped them
carry bundles and babies, while little children who could stand

on their feet had to walk endless hours. Some changed their names and lived in disguise and constant fear; and a large number, mostly the old who had felt protected by their age, were rounded up by the Germans and deported to labor camps and gas chambers.

This was to happen five years later, but at the time of our departure my worries were mixed with a certain spirit of adventure. Soon the train was in motion away from Italy.

"Nothing can stop us now," Enrico said. . . .

After our arrival in Stockholm, we were dragged into the vortex of the Nobel celebrations. There was the prize award on December 10, the anniversary of Nobel's death. Only the prizes for literature and for physics were awarded in 1938. . . .

Two weeks later we were in Southampton, where we boarded the *Franconia* for the voyage across the Atlantic, and on December 24 the children and I set out to explore the boat. As the door of the elevator swung open we were face to face with a short old man in a baggy red suit and furry white trimmings, with a long white beard and twinkling blue eyes. The three of us stood still, fascinated, open-mouthed.

The queer old man motioned us inside the elevator and then, with a benevolent smile, said to us, "Don't you know me? I am Santa Claus."

Of course, I should have known him from illustrations in English books for children. Still bewildered by my first encounter with a true Santa, I kept open-mouthed and had no words to say.

"I hope you'll be coming to my party this evening. I'll have presents for you!" Santa Claus said, bending his white beard toward my children. Their eyes sparkled. They turned to me. "Will you let us go? Please let us go!"

"Of course you may go. And thank you kindly, sir."

Later I tried to explain Santa Claus to the children. Giulio, of course, could understand little of what I said, but his eager eyes were wide open, attentive, as they always were when grown-ups were speaking.

"In each country of the world," I told them, "once a year children receive presents from a person who is not one of their parents, who comes for the sole purpose of bringing toys and candies."

"The Epiphany!" Nella interrupted.

"Yes, in Italy it is the Epiphany who comes on the sixth of January, the day the three kings brought their presents to the Child Jesus. She rides on a broom in the sky——"

"Although she is so old one can't understand how she does it," Nella put in.

"Brings toys to me, too," Giulio said. Nella turned to him.

"She has a big, big sack on her shoulders," she explained, "and when all children are asleep and it is night, she comes down the chimney, or, if there is no chimney, she enters the door and stuffs the children's stockings with toys."

"For me too," Giulio said.

"This happens in Italy. But in America there is Santa Claus. He does not ride a broomstick but a sleigh pulled by reindeer, which are animals with antlers. So he travels more comfortably and can carry a larger bag of toys. He comes once a year, the day before Christmas."

"Will the Epiphany come to us all the same? She knows we are Italian children. . . ."

"No, she will not. She could not. She could not get a visa and must remain in Italy," I answered on the inspiration of the moment.

"Poor Epiphany," Nella said wistfully. "I don't think she likes Mussolini too well."

Thus, of our own will, we had already accepted the first switch of traditions. When the *Franconia* passed the mute Statue of Liberty and entered the harbor of New York, we were already beginning to be an American family.

*   *   *

Within a year after his arrival Dr. Fermi, among other top scientists, learned that Nazi scientists in German laboratories were making frantic efforts to develop an atom bomb. This was a more deadly weapon than the world had ever known, and if the Nazis had it first they would be able to win the war in two or three knockout blows. Dr. Albert Einstein, another scientist in exile, was asked to warn President Franklin D. Roosevelt of the danger, and a highly secret research organization was set up under the code name "Manhattan Project."

From then on it was a race between Nazi scientists and those of the Free World. Enrico Fermi became head of the United States group of scientists and engineers, and their eventual success was reported by a member of the team in a coded long-distance phone call to Dr. James Conant, president of Harvard and head of National Defense Research. The conversation went something like this:

"The Italian navigator has arrived on the shores of the New World," said the scientist.

"How were the natives?" he was asked.

"Very friendly."

This coded message meant that the first atomic fire on earth had been lighted. It made the bomb possible but it also opened up a vast new source of energy which, wisely handled, could be of great benefit to mankind. Dr. Fermi, more than any other person, was responsible for its success, which is why he has been called "the father of the atomic age."

5

Refugees from Austria

In the days when Austria-Hungary was a powerful empire composed of a number of nationalities, each living in its own section of the country, all youths were pressed into military service. Karl Bitter reluctantly left his art studies in Vienna to enter the army, but after some unpleasant and unjust experiences he fled the country. In 1889, at the age of twenty-two, he arrived in the United States, where he was to become a leading sculptor. Among his noted works are the bronze doors at Trinity Church in New York City, the interior reliefs of the Penn Central Railroad station in Philadelphia, and group sculptures depicting such historic American scenes as "The Signing of the Louisiana Treaty" and "The Winning of the West."

Karl Bitter died during World War I, a war that was to bring great changes to his native land. Austria-Hungary, as an ally of Germany, shared in Germany's defeat, and the terms of surrender required that the empire be dissolved. Two new nations, Czechoslovakia and Yugoslavia, appeared for the first time on the maps of Europe. Hungary became a republic for a short period. Austria, also declared a republic, was now only a small country, without the rich agricultural regions that had belonged to Austria-Hungary. The population, reduced to six million people, found it hard to make a living during the difficult years after the war.

But Vienna, the beautiful capital where Karl Bitter had once studied, was still Vienna. Money was scarce and some of the people might have to go hungry, but something of the ancient glamour still clung to the magnificient buildings. It was still the city that had long been a center of learning, the city where Haydn, Mozart, Schubert, Beethoven, and Johann Strauss had composed unforgettable music. Brilliant men and women still made Vienna an interesting place to live, in spite of the unrest and political crises that had followed the country's fall from power.

With the rise of Hitler new dangers loomed. German Nazis, as well as Nazis in Austria who subscribed to the new political party's beliefs and prejudices, demanded an *Anschluss,* a union of the two German-speaking peoples. In March, 1938, German armies marched in and took possession of the smaller nation, and from then on the streets of Vienna and other towns resounded to the thud of Nazi boots. Red flags with the Nazi emblem, the swastika, waved from the housetops, and the only greeting permitted was "Heil Hitler!"

Many Austrians suffered during the German occupation, especially the Jews. As in Germany, they were blamed for all the troubles that had befallen their country, and this reasoning provided a convenient excuse to deprive them of their property and the businesses they had built up through the years. The terror increased as the weeks passed and more and more Jews and other anti-Nazis were deported to concentration camps. Among the Jews who escaped and took refuge in France was Franz Werfel, one of Europe's greatest writers. This proved only a temporary haven; after France was overrun by the enemy Werfel was hunted from place to place. Finally he found shelter at Lourdes, a famous Catholic shrine where he heard the story of Bernadette Soubirous. This peasant girl, he was told, had once beheld a vision of the Virgin Mary, and since that time many Catholics had visited the shrine to be healed. Franz Werfel was deeply moved.

"One day, in my distress, I made a vow," he said. "I vowed that if I escaped from this desperate situation and reached the saving shores of America, I would put aside all other tasks and sing, as best I could, the song of Bernadette."

After his arrival in the United States, Werfel fulfilled his vow, and *The Song of Bernadette* became one of his most popular books. Many other talented refugees were admitted to the United States from Austria. Usually their difficulties in adjusting to a new country were balanced by their gratitude. Probably no escapee ever felt more relieved or faced up to a new situation with more humor than did Maria August Trapp, the wife of Baron Georg von Trapp. The following selection is from her book, *The Story of the Trapp Family Singers,* basis for the famous musical and movie, *The Sound of Music.*

The First Ten Years Are the Hardest (1939)

BY MARIA AUGUSTA TRAPP

Bewildered—completely bewildered—that's what we all were when three taxis spilled us out on Seventh Avenue at 55th Street in front of the Hotel Wellington, us and our fifty-six pieces of luggage: all the instruments in their cases, the spinet, four gambas, eight recorders, the big trunks with the concert costumes, and our private belongings.

While I was standing on the sidewalk waiting for the unloading, I spelled slowly what the huge letters said: "D-R-U-G-S-T-O-R-E." It was the first time that I had met the word. In Europe we didn't have drugstores. How relieved I felt!

"That's good," I thought. "I am living in the hotel with the drugstore. I can never get lost in New York!"

The tallest houses in Vienna have five or six stories. When the elevator took us to the nineteenth floor, we simply couldn't believe it, but rushed immediately to the windows and shudderingly looked down into the deep gorge, at the bottom of which crawled little cars and tiny men. That was the first thing we reported home: "And we live on the nineteenth floor!"

The friendly gentleman from our concert manager's office who had helped us through Immigration and installed us at the hotel left us now with a friendly, "See you tomorrow."

Our last meal had been lunch on board the *American Farmer,* and by now we were all hungry. But we were not on

the boat any more, where we had just sat down to a full table
three times a day. The cruel question had to be raised now:
"How much money do we have?" After all the pockets had
been emptied, and every nickel and dime from all twelve of
us had been collected, it showed the fabulous sum of four
dollars. That had to do for supper and breakfast, and tomorrow
we would ask Mr. Wagner, our manager, for some money in
advance. The boys were sent downstairs with two dollars to
buy bread, butter, and fruit. Fresh fruit had been scarce on
board, but on land the fall is a good time to buy fruit cheaply,
and so we feasted on quantities of apples, plums, pears, and
grapes.

As we were all very tired from so much standing around
and waiting, we soon went to bed. After putting our shoes
outside the doors of our rooms, as was done in all European
hotels, we retired, only to be awakened one by one by the
night watchman, who informed us that our shoes most certainly would not be shined next morning, but they might
not be there any more, and we'd better take them in.
Funny.

Next morning I wanted my husband's hat pressed before
he appeared at the manager's office in it. To my great as-
tonishment I learned in the lobby that for this I had to go
to a shoemaker.

Georg and the boys brought back the startling news that
their shoes had been shined at the barbershop!

What a strange country!

Now I went out to look for that shoemaker to straighten
the hat. I went around the block and around another block,
and around a third block, not paying any attention to the
number of the streets. I didn't have to. Just in case I should
get lost, I knew where I belonged. It hadn't occurred to me
to remember the name of the hotel. I was so impressed by
the fact that I lived in *the* hotel with the drugstore. After
quite some searching I found my shoemaker. The hat was

pressed, but I discovered that I was completely lost. Never mind. I stepped up to the next policeman and said very politely:

"Dear Mr. Cop, where is hotel with drugstore?"

To this very day I have a tender affection for those tall New York policemen, because this one got me safely to the Wellington.

Then we went to see Mr. Wagner. The nice gentleman had come again to guide us. First we walked over to Sixth Avenue, which at that time had an elevated, also the first of its kind in our experience. I was deathly afraid, and clung tightly to Georg's arm when I had to cross the street with trains roaring over my head.

"The quickest way is the subway," and our friendly guide dived at once into a staircase, which obviously led under the street. This was really frightening. What a noise! On one side of the platform express trains thundered by, while on the other, locals came and went. The very air was in vibration, and I, simply rooted to the ground, decided not to take one single step in any direction. I was sure I would die there. Then I found myself in the inside of a howling train, from which we were spat out a few stations farther along. When we reached daylight again, I was near tears.

"Georg," I pleaded, "promise me that we will never do that again."

But before he could do so, our guide had another good idea: "This is Macy's, one of our largest department stores," he announced beamingly. "On the eighth floor they have a wonderful toy department. Let's take a quick look. The kids will like that."

And in the store we were, and for the first time in my life I was confronted with a staircase which moved by itself. First I stared at it, thinking this in itself was an exhibition piece; but when I saw people step on it and being moved upward in front of my very eyes, I got an uncomfortable feeling, as though I were witnessing witchcraft. When invited, however, to take the fatal step myself, I most vigorously declined. Meanwhile a number of people had gathered behind us. We were obviously blocking traffic.

"Go ahead, don't be silly," whispered Georg encouragingly. With a lump in my throat, I put out one foot hesitatingly, but when it touched that moving thing, I quickly drew it back as if I had been bitten by a snake. Now goodnatured, kind-hearted Americans gathered around me, and good advice from all sides made the situation more embarrassing by the second.

Behind me my little girls giggled, "Look, Mother is afraid," and I wished I had never landed on this continent.

"Close your eyes, lady, and take a step."

This was the best advice given so far. Now I was on it. How would I get off? That is easier. The staircase just slides you off, whether you want to or not. And this repeated itself seven times: "Close your eyes and take a step." Seven times? Oh no! Up to this day whenever I have to use an escalator, I close my eyes and take a deep breath.

Finally we left Macy's, and were seated in Mr. Wagner's office; and the elderly gentleman with the round, pink-cheeked, apple face looked like a very nice grandpa. We thanked him again for sending us the tickets for the *American Farmer*. He most willingly let us have money in advance. The concert tour would start in a week. So far, he had eighteen dates of the forty promised. I had difficulty in understanding him. But this I did understand when he said in parting in a very comforting tone and with a twinkle, "The first ten years are the hardest!"

Very happy, with money in our pockets, we took our leave. No, thank you, we would not need a guide any more. We had learned how terribly simple it was to get around in New York. After Fifth Avenue comes Sixth, and Seventh; and the streets are not named after flowers, birds, trees, or famous people as they are in Europe, but they are numbered.

Now we were out for a really good meal. Months ago we had learned to read a menu from right to left; and whatever it said on the menu of the hotel dining room, which was fastened inside the elevator, it cost too much. We discovered an eating place opposite the hotel called "Cafeteria." The prices were very reasonable, and the people who owned it were Chinese and very friendly.

Next morning we couldn't find Rosemarie and Lorli. They were in none of our rooms, they were not in the lobby—where could they be? After half an hour's frantic search, when we had almost reached the point of announcing to the police that they had been kidnaped, one of the bellboys came and notified us that they were riding up and down in the elevator.

"Yes, Mother," and Lorli's eyes sparkled, "up to the twenty-seventh floor. Now I can write to Susi, this is nine times as high as she lives!"

None of the people we had met on the boat lived in New York. We had no acquaintances and no friends, no letters of introduction to anybody. We discovered the New World by ourselves. We learned the difference between uptown and downtown. We found out that museums and galleries could be visited free of charge. We discovered the vast possibilities in a drugstore, where on a Sunday, when everything else was closed, you could buy anything from pencils and stationery to hot-water bottles, alarm clocks, and jewelry of any kind and description. We learned to sit at the counter with poise and order in the tone of an old-timer "Ham on rye" or "Two soft-boiled medium."

Wherever we met fellow countrymen, we learned of true adventure stories. There was, for instance, the lady who wanted to buy cauliflower.

"How much?" she asked the grocer.

"Ninety cents," was the answer.

"What?" She was outraged. "Behold your cauliflower. I can

become cauliflower myself for forty cents around the corner!"

(Such things happen when you take words from your own language and translate them into similar-sounding words in English, thinking they mean the same things. The word for "keep" in German is *behalten*, and if we want to "get" something, we say *bekommen*.)

Another incident happened to a priest friend of ours. When he first arrived in this country, he went to a parish house.

The lay brother who showed him to his quarters asked, "Is there anything else you would need, Father?"

"Well," said Father thoughtfully, "a set of new bowels every Saturday. Just hang them on the doorknob.

The lay brother seemed so startled by this request that Father had to point to a towel in his room to illustrate his wish.

Every morning we walked through the ravine of 55th Street out into Fifth Avenue and over to Saint Patrick's Cathedral, which is as large as one of the largest cathedrals of Europe; but there on the corner of 50th Street, it was overshadowed by skyscrapers. After Mass there, we walked back to the Chinese cafeteria.

We didn't want to take the little girls on the concert tour, so we looked for an inexpensive boarding school. Mr. Wagner's office helped us. We found the Ursuline Academy in the Bronx for thirty-five dollars a month apiece. For the second time in my life, I took a trip on the subway, with fingers in my ears, eyes closed for entry and exit. When we left Rosmarie and Lorli in their new school, we felt sorry for them. They had grown up in the country surrounded by meadows and trees, and there in the Bronx there was only asphalt; not a single blade of grass was to be seen. But the sisters were very nice and kind, and the children would learn English faster than we.

Once I wanted to visit the children to find out how they were doing, and in a transport of courage I walked myself down to the subway. Although I had learned that there was more than one drugstore, I had not learned that there was more than one subway line in New York. I also disregarded the warning signs "Uptown—Downtown" and felt proud to see myself finally sitting in a fast train because, so I decided, that would bring me there quicker. When the train stopped for good and all the people got out, I learned that I was far away from the Bronx. The funniest thing of all was that the subway had been metamorphosed into an elevated, and instead of walking up to the street, I had to walk down. There I was completely forlorn. But again to my rescue—a policeman. This time he was sitting in a car.

"Dear Mr. Cop Inspector," I said confidently, "help! Children in school. Bronx. How come?"

This he couldn't possibly know, but he understood me perfectly.

"You want to go there? Come on, get in my car."

We drove and drove.

All of a sudden he turned around and said:

"Tunnel, river above."

I closed my eyes, and I'm sure I went pale. What a terribly dangerous place this New York was with elevateds, escalators, subways, and tunnels. He got me safely to my Bronx convent, and the New York policemen had another jewel in their crown.

This whole trip was a mistake. When my little girls saw me, they clung to me and didn't want to let me go, crying bitterly at the final farewell so that I could hear them for more than a block. It was heartbreaking.

We really didn't need any organized sightseeing trip through New York. Every time we stepped out of the hotel it became a sightseeing tour. There were, for instance, the fire escapes, those enchanting, winding stairs outside of the houses. The trolleycars and the buses were different from the ones at home. There were newsstands with so terrifically many different papers and magazines, and the newspapers themselves of the size of sheets for a baby's bed. Enchanted, we watched men climbing on something like a throne and cute little boys falling over their shoes in a holy fury until they were as shiny as mirrors—and this right on the street! Why didn't people all stop and watch? Well, and then the people! There were Negroes—men, women, and children. Oh, what cute children! There were Chinese people—maybe they were Japanese, one didn't know. Most of them talked English, but we also heard Italian and German, Yiddish and Greek. And there was the climate. Although it was now October, it was hot and damp, quite different from Salzburg. Then there was the speed. What an experience to go down Broadway for the first time when the movies were over. What a noise, what light, what a rush; or to cross Fifth Avenue around noon, or Wall Street at five o'clock. All this first and most overwhelming sightseeing in New York didn't cost much. It was thrilling and frightening—it was wonderful and terrible—these first steps into a new continent: *our* discovery of America!

My mind was stubbornly set on learning English. I read every advertisement in subways, on buses, on street corners, and in elevators. I memorized the menus and, with the help of a small dictionary, started to read a copy of *The Reader's Digest*.

I invented a method all my own, in which I wanted to apply what I had learned about one word to as many like-sounding words as I could find. This proved later to be fatally wrong, and it still haunts my English of today. For instance, I had learned: "freeze—frozen." I wrote underneath in my precious little notebook: "squeeze—squozen," and "sneeze—snozen." Proudly I talked about someone being a "thunkard," explaining wordily that I had thought if drinking much makes a person a drunkard, then thinking much, like that professor I had in mind, makes him a "thunkard." When I admired the tall "hice" in New York, I got quite offended because they seemed to overlook the logical similarity between "mouse—mice" and "house—hice." I talked about the "reet" of my teeth, feeling perfectly correct in doing so. Wasn't it "foot—feet," after all ?

Especially is it bad if you translate the Bible literally. The effect was tremendous when I informed a group of people with whom I had come to talk in the lobby that "the ghost was willing, but the meat was soft."

But what a triumph you have after so much trouble and work, after so many unexpected fits of laughter, after hours of spelling and learning by heart, when one day the nice Negro elevator operator says to you, "Ma'am, your English is getting better every day."

From then on you can hardly discover any trace of an accent in your speech. You feel rewarded for all the blood, sweat, and tears of the last weeks' English battle.

Then comes the great day when you feel like graduating. The man at the desk asks you sincerely and confidently, "How many years did you study English before you came to this country, Madam?"

Mr. Wagner must have made a mistake when he said, "The first ten years are the hardest." He must have meant the first ten *days!*

6

Refugees from Germany

The first formal protest against black slavery in America was made by a group of German refugees nearly three centuries ago. These people, members of a religious sect known as Mennonites who founded Germantown, in Pennsylvania, were distressed to learn that many Negroes were actually owned by the white race. "Here [in America] is liberty of conscience," read a resolution adopted by the Mennonites in 1688, "which is right and reasonable. Here ought to be likewise liberty of the body."

Members of several other religious groups that had been persecuted in Germany accepted William Penn's invitation to make their homes in Pennsylvania. They and other German settlers gradually spread out into the other colonies, and by the time the American Revolution began about one tenth of the colonial population was of German birth or descent. Many of the soldiers under General Washington were children and grandchildren of refugees and helped to win independence for a new nation dedicated to the cause of freedom.

In Germany the situation was quite different. It was not a real nation at that time but a collection of separate states in which the poor were oppressed by the unprincipled rulers. Francis Lieber, one patriotic Prussian student who urged reform, was arrested by a reactionary Prussian government as a dangerous radical. Since the only evidence against him was a collection of poems and essays he had written about liberty, he was never brought to trial, but he came to the conclusion that there was no chance for democracy in Germany. He fled to England and later, in 1827, to the United States.

"I do not expect a paradise," he wrote to his family, "but I look forward to the prospect of . . . an honorable and useful position in a young republic which, however imperfect it may still be, yet gives a field for . . . talent and ability."

His expectations were more than realized. Much that he had hoped for in his native land had already been accomplished in America, where even working people were better off than in Europe. As the years passed he taught in several universities, took an active part in the antislavery movement, and edited the *Encyclopedia Americana*.

In the years that followed, other Germans who shared Francis Lieber's ideas became naturalized citizens of the United States. Carl Schurz, one of the "Forty-eighters" who escaped from Germany after the failure of the Revolution of 1848, was the first American of foreign birth to serve in the United States Senate, after which he was Secretary of the Interior. He brought about needed reforms in the treatment of the Indians and, as a writer, had a wide following both in his adopted and in his native land. Many dissatisfied Germans, after reading his books and articles, decided to throw in their lot with the United States.

Though Germany had become a united nation in 1871, the government was still oppressive, and each upheaval there, each period of unrest, provided the United States with some more fine citizens. Never was this more true than after 1933, the year Adolf Hitler, the Nazi Führer, came to power. All too many Germans, left poor and disheartened by their defeat in World War I, had been ready to listen to the glib promises of a powerful orator. Too late, they realized the evil of his plans, when Germany became a police state and dissenters were cruelly punished. Many fled to avoid arrest. Others, including such famous Germans as Thomas Mann, Nobel Prize winner for literature, and members of his talented family, left because they found life intolerable under the Nazis. Paul Tillich, for example, a member of the faculty of Union Seminary in New York City and one of America's best known Protestant theologians, had once been dismissed from his post in Munich because he opposed the brutal policies of the new government.

Though both Catholics and Protestants were persecuted under the Nazis, the worst atrocities were directed against the Jews. Hitler made them the scapegoat, attributing to them all the difficulties that had grown out of Germany's defeat in World War I. Before the nightmare ended with Hitler's suicide, at least six million Jews, more than three fourths of the total Jewish population, had been killed or had died under horrible conditions in Nazi concentration camps.

Others lucky enough to escape and come to America included distinguished artists, musicians, writers, teachers, and scientists. Albert Einstein, whose theory of relativity was to revolutionize scientific thought, was also a great human being who believed that there was "no higher religion than human service." Many others were also able to rise above bitterness and find new and meaningful careers in the United States. Such a man was Dr. Fred S. Sondermann, who became a professor of political science at Colorado State College. The following account deals primarily with a visit he made to the places where he had lived as a boy. His story has been adapted and condensed from his journal and from a sermon delivered at the Temple Beth El in Colorado Springs shortly after he returned to his adopted country.

Refugee's Return (1939)

BY FRED S. SONDERMANN

A former German Jew who returns to Germany after thirty years carries with him a difficult legacy. It is not necessary to dwell on the incredible barbarities and cruelties that were inflicted on fellow Jews by the Nazis in the thirties and forties, resulting in the virtual elimination through genocide of the Jewish communities of Germany and of the other parts of Europe that fell under Nazi domination. Many members of my own and my wife's families—grandparents, uncles, aunts, cousins, as well as many good friends—were the victims of the greatest organized crime wave in all recorded history, which must forever be part of the record we transmit to our children.

In September, 1969, I spent the better part of a week in

Horn, the small town where I had lived until I was thirteen and where my family had lived since the middle of the eighteenth century, and probably even before that. When I visited there I met many former friends with whom I had played as a child until they could no longer afford to be seen with me and had to drop the relationship. I could sense that many of them felt there was an implicit question in our reunion: had I forgiven them, could I forgive them, for the ostracism to which I was subjected in those days? I think that the answer to this has to be yes. Children can be thoughtless and cruel all on their own, of course; but in this case I do not see how they really had adequate defenses against a system that prescribed certain behaviors to them.

It was a strange sensation to drive back into the town after such a long time away. With my wife, Marion, our two sons, and our daughter, I drove right to the *Marktplatz*, the central square, parked the car, and stood in front of "our" house. It was much as it had been thirty-two years ago, and I just stood and looked at it for a while before we went into the hotel, which is also located in the square. I introduced myself to the owner, who had once been my playmate, and then we settled down in three comfortable, pleasant, and cheap rooms in the remodeled hotel. The original part of the city was much the same, except that everything seemed much smaller and distances less than I remembered from my childhood. The city, like almost all old German cities, was once surrounded by a wall, parts of which are still standing. There is also the old castle, which is now used as a local museum. I visited the building in which the old synagogue had been located. At the time I grew up, there were only five Jewish families left in town, and only two children—a girl, Hilde Blank, who died in a concentration camp, and myself.

I had been an only child, born in 1923. Yet though our immediate family was small, the "extended" family was very close. Our household consisted of my parents and me and always one of my two grandmothers. There were uncles and aunts and cousins who frequently came to visit, and I felt as if I belonged to a very large and nice family.

We were not wealthy, but there was always enough to go around. My father had a small store—Men's and Women's Clothing. The store occupied about half of the downstairs of the house in which we lived. My parents led a harmonious life. Hardly a Sunday passed that friends did not drop in for dinner or a cold supper. We took many trips, to various resorts and to visit grandparents who lived in a small village about forty miles away, where they had a lovely new house and a big garden where I could pick strawberries for breakfast.

There were other trips to visit other members of the family, especially to Düsseldorf, and in the later 1930s I usually spent my summers with cousins in Holland. Since I came from the state where Prince Bernhard, the husband of the then Crown Princess Juliana, had been born, and since I had gone to school with his cousin, Prince Armin, I remember being quite the "big cheese" among my Dutch friends.

I started school in 1929. One of my first memories was an Assembly to celebrate the departure of the last French troops from the German Rhineland. We heard patriotic speeches and sang "Die Wacht Am Rhein"—The Watch on the Rhine—in honor of the occasion. I can still hear it. Years later, in 1953, on the evening before I received my Ph.D. from Yale, Marion and I went to a concert of the Glee Club, and one of their selections was the same song which I had sung on one of my first days in school. It had different lyrics, of course, but it struck me as a strange coincidence that my formal education should be bounded on both ends by this particular melody.

I must have gone to the regular *Volks-Schule* for four years, until I was ten. Then I was sent to a small private school, the *Rektorschule*. By now we were well into the 1930s. I remember the day Hitler took power, January 30, 1933, because it was the same day my grandmother Elise Sondermann died. Her funeral a few days later was an impressive event: the horse-drawn funeral cortege with hundreds of people walking behind it, my dad and I in the front row. My grandmother had been an institution in the community. One thing I remember about her were the literally dozens of baskets of food which she prepared each Christmas for the poor people in the town. I had to help our maids deliver them in person. My mother kept this up a couple of years after 1933, but later the bad times were upon us, and the custom was discontinued.

I also recall coming home from a school excursion a couple of months later to see people standing in front of our store. My dad had been forced to put a sign in the display window to the effect, "Don't buy from me. This is a Jewish store." The business steadily declined. By 1936 and 1937, there were days when not a single customer entered the store. My mother thought we should stay put anyhow, that the madness could not last. My dad thought otherwise, and finally, in 1937, we left Horn and moved to an apartment in Cologne, which we shared with an elderly uncle and aunt of my mother. I don't know what we lived on in those years. Perhaps there were some savings, but in any event there was no job for my dad. It was a difficult time.

In 1937, when I was thirteen, I left school with no regrets. After my close friends, Joe and Karl Meyer, left, first for Holland and later for America, I was the only Jewish student in a school of more than 600, most of them members of the Hitler Youth. On one occasion when I won first prize in an essay contest, I was asked to withdraw my entry, because the prize simply could not be given to a Jew. But I would just as soon not dwell on such experiences now.

After moving to Cologne, I took some private lessons in English and French. Then I was sent to Munich, where I spent a year living with a Jewish widow whose husband had been killed at the Dachau concentration camp. She had a lovely apartment, overlooking the Isar River. I spent my days and most of my evenings learning to cook in a Jewish cooking school. The idea of training me to be a cook was that in our attempt to emigrate it would help to know a trade.

Later I became an apprentice in a Jewish "pension." It was in a building next to the Roonstrasse synagogue, and in November, 1938, that synagogue—like all others in Germany —was burned in retaliation for the shooting of a German embassy official in Paris by a young Polish Jew. I had gone to work that morning, not knowing what had happened. During the day, a crowd gathered, the synagogue burned, and there was the possibility that the adjacent house where I was working would also be burned. I escaped over a back fence and ran toward home, pursued by some young Nazis. But I managed to get into a taxi and reached home safely.

Though my family for a number of years had tried to emigrate from Germany, it was not as easy as it sounds. At first my dad was anxious not to lose everything he had. Not that we had all that much, but we managed to live rather comfortably. He made a trip to Italy and came back with a proposition to "buy into" a factory in Milan. Then it appeared that about half of his belongings would be confiscated by the German government if he went through with that project, so the plan was abandoned. Another time Dad traveled to Holland to see what business connections he might make there, but nothing came of it.

In retrospect, of course, I have much reason to be grateful that the project failed. All my relatives who had moved to Holland were overtaken by the German invasion of 1940 and eventually transported to extermination camps, where they were killed. Surely this would also have happened to us, had we gone there.

At last we concentrated on going to the United States, and Dad got a friend in Holland to put up $10,000 as a guarantee that we would not be a burden on the American public. (The understanding was, of course, that we would never touch the

money, and we never did.) Even so, getting out of Germany
was a slow process, because the American quota of some 35,-
000 German immigrants per year was heavily oversubscribed
with Jews trying to leave. We had to wait two and a half or
three years before our quota number was even called up.

I remember traveling to the American Consulate in Stuttgart and waiting interminably in long lines to be questioned
and examined. Finally my parents and I were given visas, but
not my maternal grandmother who had intended to emigrate
with us. It was a hard decision to make, and my mother never
got over it. My grandmother had to stay behind, and in the end
she suffered the same fate as every other member of my family
who was not able to get out.

After our visas were granted in the early summer of 1939,
we purchased tickets for the U.S.S. *Manhattan*, which was to
leave from Hamburg in early September. August was a nervous month, with ever-increasing warlike gestures on the part
of the Nazi government. The announcement of the Nazi-
Soviet nonaggression pact came like a bombshell, and the
meaning was perfectly clear. On August 25 the movers came
to pack our furniture for the overseas transport, but we would
never receive it. It got as far as Rotterdam, where it was
bombed. My dad decided we could not risk waiting any longer.
Because of recent events, it seemed unlikely that any American ship would come to Hamburg in early September, and he
managed to secure transit visas at both the Belgian and French
consulates. Then on the afternoon of August 26, while the
packers were still in the house, we took our suitcases, said the
difficult goodbyes to Grandmother, Uncle, and Aunt, and took
the streetcar to the main railroad station to board an agoniz-
ingly slow train to the border.

At Aachen, the border station, we had to change trains, and
while we waited for the one to take us to Belgium, an SS man
in his black uniform came to inquire about our mission. He had
all of us thoroughly examined, and my dad was confined for

nearly an hour. Everything seemed to hang in the balance, and when he finally reappeared he never said what had transpired. At last we were on the train and across the Belgian border. I understand that the border was sealed soon afterward.

After a day or two in Paris and one in LeHavre, we caught the ship in the latter port. My dad had been right: the *Manhattan* never made it to Hamburg. We were on the high seas, somewhere southwest of Ireland, when war was declared. We arrived in New York with one suitcase apiece and with German marks amounting to about $4.

Though I had been afraid to make the return visit to Horn, I found it an enriching experience. I was particularly pleased to find how many of the people remembered my parents and how highly they spoke of them. I saw many friends and acquaintances from former days. One of them, Rudy Rose, was the only one who explicitly asked me how I had really felt back in those years when all my friends, one after the other, had to drop me. He had often thought about it and wondered whether I had been able to forgive him and the others. (Later, when I had written him a note from Munich which I signed "Your friend Fred," I received a very touching reply, thanking me for reviving the former friendship.)

An old teacher, Mr. Reineking, now in his eighties, came to the hotel to meet me. He told me how he had been involved, as an arbitrator or factfinder, in a situation involving my dad's business. The wife of the local clergyman had been reported as still trading in a Jewish store, by some Nazi who claimed to have seen her come out of our front door. She denied it, and he, the teacher, was appointed to find out the truth of the matter. He extricated her and himself by "finding" that the charge was unprovable, that the person who had submitted the report had stood in a spot from where one could not clearly see from which of a number of doors a person was emerging.

My wife, Marion, found it an incredible story and was quite

turned off by it. Why hadn't he simply said that it was nobody's business where anyone did her shopping? I have somewhat more sympathy with his predicament and that of all others who had been similarly involved—and caught.

When we left Horn on a Saturday morning, the owner of the hotel came to see us off. Friends brought bags of candy and fruit to see us through the day's journey. How different was this second exodus from the town of my birth from the first! I remembered how that first time, I had boarded the streetcar in front of our house. I had looked back at the house as long as I could, wondering if I would ever see it again. I had not said goodbye to anyone, and no one had said goodbye to me.

I am trying not to become maudlin about the Germans, particularly about those of the war and the pre-war generation. Their government, in their name (if not always with their approval), committed some of the most terrible crimes recorded in human history. My boys and I visited the Dachau concentration camp and spent a sobering morning there. I felt this was necessary for their education and also for mine. Yet, as we approached it, I felt a terrible reluctance to go through with the visit. Then I felt ashamed of myself, when so many people had had no choice, and must have known that they would never come out alive.

Dachau today contains an excellent museum and the most impressive sculpture—of men caught in barbed wire—that I have ever seen. But for the rest of it, it is quite impossible today to recapture the horror which it must once have been. The crematorium also still stands, and it takes a great effort to force oneself to enter it. It is surrounded by mass graves, now beautifully landscaped. A Protestant chapel, a Catholic chapel with adjoining convent, and a Jewish chapel complete the complex of what was the first major concentration camp in Germany.

I also visited the spot in the city of Detmold on which had once stood the synagogue in which I had my Bar Mitzvah in 1936. Like all other synagogues, it was destroyed in the "Crystal Night" of 1938. Now a small park occupies the site, and a plaque is inscribed with a quotation from the prophet Malachi which had once been inscribed over the front door of the old building: "Have we not all one Father? Hath not one God created us? Why, then, do we deal treacherously brother against brother and destroy the bond which God has created?"

In spite of these personal moments, I was clearly an outsider, clearly a different person than when I had left Germany as a youth. I think this situation gives me some of the detachment necessary to appraise the difficult question of a Jew's attitude toward Germany today. One cannot forget what happened. The record is too enormous to allow such an easy escape. Yet one can remember that most Germans suffered enormously. Proportionately, Jews endured more than others, but Dachau contained as many or more non-Jews as Jews. Too, I was struck by the enormous destruction of property and, more importantly, of life and health which was the price the Germans—Nazis and non-Nazis alike—had to pay for the misdeeds of their government, their society, themselves. We can at least be conscious of this fact.

One must also make distinctions among Germans. A number of them fought courageously against the regime, usually with fatal consequences. A larger number were appalled but felt helpless. Some, of course, were wholeheartedly in support of what was done. It is no longer easy—it may not even any longer be possible—to disentangle exactly who did what and why in those years. But surely the young generation now in their twenties and thirties cannot be burdened with whatever guilt their parents must carry.

Then, it seems to me that Jews, of all people, should eschew the practice of ascribing to groups the characteristics of individuals. This is precisely what the Nazis did to them. I know that there are extremist elements in Germany which worry me; just as there are in this country where, at the moment, they worry me even more. But I also feel that the traumatic experience through which the Germans have come has given a better chance than ever before for creating a more decent, humane, just, and sensitive society. It is an act of self-interest, and also one of justice and charity, to encourage those elements in the German society which are moving toward such a future.

7

Refugees from England

The first refugees in America were the settlers in Plymouth, Massachusetts, more than three and a half centuries ago. Now called Pilgrims, because they had come on a pilgrimage to seek religious freedom, they were the vanguard of a great migration. The Puritans who followed the Pilgrims came for the same reason, to escape persecution for their religious beliefs, but oddly enough they themselves persecuted those who disagreed with them. Settlers in Boston, Salem, and other New England towns were obliged to attend Puritan churches and subscribe to Puritan dogma. Those who objected, in turn, had to become refugees.

The best-known among them was Roger Williams, outspoken young pastor of the church in Salem. He preached that it was wrong to persecute a man because of his convictions, and for holding such a "dangerous opinion" the magistrates of the colony ordered him banished. It was winter and bitter cold as he made his way through the wilderness to the wigwam of some Indian friends. The following spring he founded the town of Providence in what was to become the colony of Rhode Island. Here many of the dissatisfied people from Massachusetts and also from old England were made welcome, regardless of what religion they professed.

Meanwhile, Lord Baltimore had founded Maryland primarily for Roman Catholics who had been harassed by authorities in the British government, though the colony was also open to persons of other faiths. A half century later William Penn founded Pennsylvania as a haven for the persecuted members of the Society of Friends, or Quakers, but the population was never limited to Quakers or to

Englishmen. People of all religions and from other European countries were urged to make their homes in what he wanted to be "a free
colony for all mankind." Some of his ideas about liberty, as did those
of Roger Williams, later found a place in the Declaration of Independence when the United States became a nation.

The same ideas were influential in England, which, as more and
more years passed, became a bastion for freedom and democracy. In
our own twentieth century, many victims of Bolshevik terror during
the Russian Revolution and, later, of Nazi persecution in Germany
found asylum in Britain. During World War II when the Nazis overran Poland and several other European countries, there was an even
greater influx of refugees. Members of the governments of several
conquered nations set up governments-in-exile in London, and thousands of young men from those same countries escaped to England.
Here they joined the Allies in waging the war to bring freedom to
their homelands.

Though the English lived under constant threat of invasion, they
made heroic efforts to care for the refugees that crowded their small
island. After the Nazis began frequent bombings in 1940, many English boys and girls were evacuated to Canada and the United States.
One Englishman active in the movement to send children to a land
where they would be safe was Kenneth Bell, a teacher of history at
Oxford University. Among the earliest arrivals in America were several members of his own family: Caroline, Eddie, and their elder
sister, Mrs. Laurence Montague, with her three small children. At
the suggestion of an American writer, Alden Hatch, Caroline, aged
twelve, and Eddie, ten, dictated their impressions to Mrs. Montague.
The following excerpt is from their book, *Thank You Twice.*

How We Like America (1940)

BY CAROLINE AND EDDIE BELL

When we rolled up to the big white wooden house near New
Milford, Connecticut, that became our American home, we

pretty well filled it up. We brought the number of English refugees it harbored up to eight, six of whom were Bells. The other two, Kate and Amy, were Jewish and our hosts, the four D'Altons, were Roman Catholic. Then there was Jessie, a big black woman who did the heavy work and was Baptist. But, because it was nearby, all of us except the D'Altons went to the little white church with a thin high spire, which is Methodist. This must be what we heard people call the American Melting Pot. . . .

Naturally we knew that the Indians were all killed off in the eastern part of America, but in this house we seem closer to them than we thought we would. You see, it is over two hundred years old, which is pretty old for America—lots of our English houses are over five hundred years old. It was built by the pioneers out of the forest that stood here. You can see the marks of their axes on the beams of the dining-room ceiling.

The chipped places on the dark old beams seem to make those chaps real. Before, they were just something you read about in history, like the ancient Greeks.

The D'Altons told us what fun the settlers used to have at what they called a "house raising." They would gather from miles around to help put the great timbers in place, and afterward they'd have a tremendous feast with all sorts of things to eat like turkey and pumpkin pies. They must have been very jolly parties and were probably the start of the American habit of "getting together."

But the best thing about the house is a little hidey-hole between the fireplaces, which are back to back. This is where they used to put the women and children when the Indians went on the warpath and attacked the farms. They'd be quite safe there while the men were popping away at the Indians through loopholes in the heavy wooden shutters.

Even if the Indians took the farm, they'd never guess there was such a place, and if they burned the house down the women and children would still be protected by all the bricks, the D'Altons say; but we think they might have been pretty well roasted.

It must have been great fun being a pioneer. Even on the dullest jobs, like hoeing corn, you never could tell when an arrow would go whooshing by and you'd have to grab your gun and run for the house. It's lucky the Indians weren't as good shots as Robin Hood and his merry men or America might never have got settled.

(That's Eddie. He may think fighting Indians was exciting, but I don't think it was much fun for the women and children shut up in that dark little hole. It was too much like being in an air raid shelter with Nazis overhead.—C.B.)

Although the house is so old, it has the usual modern conveniences that Americans simply can't live without. There are two bathrooms, one of which has a shower bath. Showers *are* a convenience because you can get a clean look in about two minutes when a grown-up person tells you that you are looking simply filthy. There are twelve of us in the house altogether, so two bathrooms are jolly nice to have. At home we had one for about the same number of people and that meant queueing up in front of the door. The shower and all the hot water is grand, but all the same, Americans expect you to do an awful lot of washing. In fact it's a wonder some of their children aren't washed away entirely. . . .

Now we will tell you about our hosts and friends, the D'Altons. There are four of them: Mrs. D'Alton and her three sons. Bill is the youngest of the boys. He is about sixteen, tall and dark. He talks all the time in a funny way so you never know when he is serious. When he isn't talking he plays the piano and sings, or bangs like fury on his drum. American boys seem to be allowed to make an awful lot of noise.

Bill works hard. He had a job on the farm most of the summer and got up early and toiled all day at getting in the tobacco and corn crop. He and Eddie helped to fill the silo and Bill got paid for this work. (I think it's a jolly good idea for boys to be able to earn some money in the holidays. They hardly ever do in England.—E.B.)

Bob is the next one, twenty. He works as a surveyor in the State Highway Department and is very keen on his job. He knows a lot of things besides, and explains everything so clearly that Eddie can understand about such things as car engines, water works, and the oil furnace. He is best of all the D'Altons at answering questions.

(The great things about Bob is that he *does* things. I think it's sensible to stop going to college for a while and find out about things by doing them. At Oxford the undergraduates just sit around and read books and play games. So I think I should like to go to an American college. But I must find out more about them first.—E.B.)

Jack, the eldest, is studying to be a doctor. He is quieter than the others and seems a bit stand-offish—his mother says he is just like an Englishman. But he is grand fun when you get to know him.

You can see why we like living with the D'Altons. All of them, and we refugees, gather around a big table for supper and talk about all the things that have happened during the day.

Bob comes clumping in, looking very tough in his black-and-red checked wool shirt and riding breeches. "Wow!" he says. "Did we have a day! Oh, Momma, the road sure was icy!"

It's awfully funny to hear a big man say, "Oh, Momma."

Bob has marvelous adventures. One Sunday he went driving in a State Police car that was all lined with concrete and had guns hidden in it, just like in the American films. And a two-way radio to talk to headquarters!

Bob told us how they got word of an accident and roared off at seventy miles an hour.

"We got there just as they were lifting the hurt folks into the ambulance," he said. "Cars and people were strewn all over the road. We got in front of the ambulance and ripped along ahead of them with the siren going like mad to clear the way. Holy Mike, we were traveling! We got those folks to the hospital in jig time."

"I wish I'd been with you," Eddie said. "It must have been exciting."

"It sure was," said Bob. "That road was sure a bloody mess."

All we English gasped. Then Eddie asked Bob if he knew what *bloody* means.

"It means bloody to me," said Bob. "What's it mean to you?"

"In England it's the most awful swearword there is."

"This really was bloody," insisted Bob. "Honest-to-goodness blood!"

That's the way Bob talks. Wow! You sure do start talking that way too if you don't watch out. It's lucky there are six other English people in the house so we can hear *English* English spoken.

At supper, we Bells match Bob's stories with good tales about Father and his queer doings; and particularly how he rules the conversation at the table. If anyone gets into a long story that is frightfully dull, Father says, "That's irrelevant. Leave it out." And you have to shut up or keep to the point.

Mrs. D'Alton thoroughly approved of this, and when she found that we had a rather stern-looking picture of Father, with his hair unnaturally smooth, she brought it down and set it on the table.

"There," she said. "Your father can keep you in order now."

We got out a very jolly picture of Father laughing, with his hair standing straight on end, and put it beside the other one. Then, if there was a good joke, we could say Father was enjoying it too.

We hadn't been in America more than a day or two before we had to go to school. We had no idea what it would be like except what Bill D'Alton told us; and he was plainly pulling our legs with a lot of wild stories.

At eight-ten that morning we were at the gate waiting for the school bus. It was early September and very hot, so we had on thin clothes. Our legs were bare and we wore sand shoes. It was not at all like starting the autumn term in England, where Eddie, for instance, wore a stuffy school uniform of gray flannel shorts, jacket and shirt and gray stockings. The rolled-down stocking tops were red and green to match his tie and cap.

We had heard that American schools were very modern with wonderful buildings; and so they are. But the school buses —or at least that one—were not at all new. We started off, and such a banging and clattering you never heard. The dirt road was full of holes, and the jolly old bus just leaped from one to the next with a series of terrific crashes. Then it stopped to take in several boys. One of them was dressed in pale green pajamas with the jacket hanging out! From there on the bus kept stopping and soon it was full of children.

When it was jammed so full it could just barely groan along, the bus got to New Milford. We hadn't been there before, and we loved it. There were white houses all along the pretty village green and tall trees with leaves like lace. The bus stopped at a schoolhouse on the green. All the smaller children got out. The older ones tried to push us out too, but we kept shouting, "Is this right for the seventh and eighth grades?" We had been told beforehand we were to be in those grades.

One of the big boys said, "No, this is the grammar school, but you can't possibly be in junior high."

Eddie was not yet ten and did look rather small. But we resolutely stuck to our guns, and finally got to the high school.

(My small size is a great nuisance to me at school. Girls are always looking at me and saying, "How cute," and big boys come up and say, "If anyone starts a fight with you, call me and I'll fix them." They mean it most kindly, but of course I wouldn't dream of doing such a thing.—E.B.)

The high school was all the things that the bus wasn't: big

and modern and made of brick with three floors. The class-rooms had fine, large windows, and desks for about forty children in each. There were interesting pictures on the walls above the blackboards, which ran around three sides of the rooms.

We were in a fearful muddle that first day. We had to find the different rooms for our classes, which was confusing to us because in England you sit still and the classes come to you, that is the teachers do. The lessons seemed to last hardly any time at all, and every time the sharp electric bells went off we jumped into the air. (There are no school bells in England any more because they were always being confused with air raid warnings and alarms to say the Nazis were invading England. —C.B.)

As soon as we got used to the school we found it far easier than at home. We had only history, geography, arithmetic, and English in junior high; at home we had eight subjects. Then, too, things went very slowly because there were so many in the classes; but it wasn't quite as easy as it looked, for once you knew a thing, you were supposed to remember it always. Eddie was delighted to find that we were not having Latin until we are older.

There is a peculiar collection of children in our grades. They are of all ages and sizes. There are a lot of children with names ending in "ski" or "ska," whose parents came from Poland and Czechoslovakia, and others from Sweden, Italy, and Germany. In one class the teacher asked if any of the children had both parents of the same nationality, and out of a class of thirty-five only three raised their hands.

The children asked us some very silly questions, such as "What language do they speak in England?" (Maybe they were what they call "kidding" us.—C.B.) At first they were very envious about us because they knew we were refugees, but when they found we hadn't been bombed and had no horrible stories to tell, they gave up and treated us just like ordinary people, only occasionally shouting about America being the best country in the world—in case we should forget.

The American schools go in heavily for patriotism. We started the day by saluting the flag and gabbling a lot of words which we didn't understand until later when we saw them written. Part of it sounded like "routine and justice for all," and we thought Mother would approve of that, because she is such a one for routine (It's "liberty and justice."—C.B.), and another part sounded like *République française,"* which seemed odd, until we learned that it really was "Republic for which it stands."

They don't have all this patriotic business with Union Jacks and "God Save the King" in England. We wondered why it is necessary over here, and decided that it's because the parents of the children come from so many different countries that the school teachers want to make them sure they are Americans and nothing else; and make them proud of it.

They have another thing that you don't get in English schools, and it's a jolly good idea. That is this League business. We were told that we should belong to the Junior Citizenship League (even though we are not citizens). They have masses of committees, so everybody is sure to be on one, at least. It's grand when a chap gets up and bangs on the table with a little wooden hammer and says in a businesslike voice, "Meeting called to order." All Americans, even children, love to organize things, and the things they organize at school are jolly good fun sometimes.

For instance, they arranged a grand party at Halloween. We had been a little disappointed when we found they didn't celebrate Guy Fawkes day here in November and that we should have to wait until the Fourth of July for fireworks. (November fifth is the day Guy Fawkes did *not* blow up the Houses of Parliament. In England in peacetime we burn an old Guy made of old clothes on a huge bonfire. Then we let off masses of fireworks and rush about making lots of noise in the dark. Of course, the war stopped the fireworks, and now we find that children aren't allowed to set off fireworks in America even in peacetime.—C.B.) But then along came Halloween, and we were allowed to dress up in funny clothes and do all sorts of mad things.

Our grade organized a fancy-dress party. Mrs. D'Alton gave Eddie an old costume of her son Bill's. It had been George Washington, but she turned it into a Chinaman costume by putting long black stockings on it and tying them around the trousers with tape. Instead of George Washington's cocked hat, Eddie wore an old sewing basket with a pigtail stitched to it, and a terrifying Chinese mask. Caroline was a scarecrow in huge old clothes and sticks in her long sleeves for hands; and immense old shoes over her slippers.

We had a marvelous time and ate masses of doughnuts and drank sweet cider until we felt absolutely bottled. It was all due to a little organization and only cost five cents!

A few weeks later we plunged into Christmas preparations. There were lots of packages to wrap and the tree to trim. We all had presents for each other, and there were mysterious packages also. For the Americans had been very nice to us and, besides sending us presents, had given us extra money to buy presents for the people we liked.

It was all finished by Christmas Eve, and we decided to go to the carol singing. It was a lovely, frosty night with no moon but lots of stars; the air was crisp and electric, and yet peaceful. As we got near the village, we began to pass little lighted Christmas trees in front of the pretty white houses. We had never seen any before as there are none outdoors in England. They were so lovely, sparkling out happiness and Christmas feeling. Some were all blue and some were green and red, and others were all colors; but all of them were pretty.

The main street of New Milford was absolutely lined with the gay trees and looked like a picture. We wandered around the village looking at the lighted trees and singing carols as we went. We bellowed out "Good King Wenceslaus" and other old familiar English songs. When we ran out of carols, we started on hymns. Of course we thought of England, and the blackness over it, and the people we loved there. But we all hid from each other what we were thinking, and at least the Nazis had promised not to bomb that night.

Christmas Day was great fun. We all had stockings, and had filled one for Jessie, the fat cheerful black woman, and hung it on her door. She had not taken it in when we got up at seven o'clock, so Caroline opened the door. Jessie gave a shriek, and Caroline threw the stocking at her, shouting, "It's from Father Christmas."

After breakfast we had fun playing with our new toys, and the D'Alton boys enjoyed it as much as we did. Bob, the engineer, built a magnificent crane, that really worked, with our nephew Donald's new Erector set. Jack and Eddie got the new electric train roaring around in a shower of sparks. Bill D'Alton set up all the model airplanes and amused our big sister's baby by making dive-bombing attacks with tremendous buzzes and roars.

We had a huge turkey for dinner. People kept dropping in and Mrs. D'Alton thoughtfully served tea, to give an English air. In spite of being so far away from home, and being just a little worried about people there, we did have a happy Christmas.

When we go back, I think the thing we will love most and remember best about America is this Christmas; and especially the little lighted Christmas trees. They make you feel that Americans don't want to keep their Christmas happiness just to themselves, but wish everyone to have a part of it. That gives you a warm and happy feeling.

When we do go back, we plan to take the necessary things with us and light an outdoor tree in England.

8

Norwegian Refugees

"The Norwegian Mayflower," as Americans of Norwegian descent think of it, was a sloop known as the *Restaurationen* in 1825. The forty-six passengers disembarking in New York were Quakers who felt persecuted after they had left the official Lutheran Church in their native land. They were seeking refuge in a country whose Constitution guaranteed freedom of religion, but their first settlement on the shores of Lake Ontario proved to be a disappointment to some of the colonists. One of them, Cleng Peerson, determined to seek a better location farther west, walked a thousand miles until he reached the new state of Illinois. There, on the banks of the Fox River, he found what he considered the ideal location and persuaded some of his friends back east to establish another colony in a new Promised Land.

Those early refugees were the forerunners of thousands of immigrants, not only from Norway but from neighboring Sweden. Neither was the progressive nation that it is today, but by the time World War II began no countries in the world were more democratic. When the Nazis invaded Scandinavia in 1940, Sweden was spared and welcomed thousands of refugees who fled from Nazi-occupied Norway, Denmark, and Holland. Many remained for the duration; others left from there for the United States.

The Norwegians have a long tradition of peace, but they proved they loved freedom even more when they were treacherously attacked. The people put up a fierce resistance, but theirs was a small country and in two months it was completely occupied by the enemy. A puppet government was set up, with Vidkun Quisling, a

Norwegian who had cooperated with the Nazis, named as premier. Since then the word "quisling" has been considered a synonym for "traitor."

Meanwhile, when King Haakon VII realized that surrender was inevitable, he fled to London and set up a government-in-exile. Crown Prince Olaf joined him there, and thousands of other young men left Norway in open boats to join new military forces being trained in England and later in Canada. Among the exiles who sought refuge in the United States were Crown Princess Martha, a future queen of Norway, her three royal children, and Sigrid Undset.

Mrs. Undset, one of Norway's greatest novelists and winner of the Nobel Prize for literature, was in Oslo, the capital, the night of April 9, 1940, when it was learned that the country had been invaded. Her older son Anders joined up at once with the Norwegian armed forces, the younger boy Hans joined the ambulance corps, and she returned to her home at Lillehammer. She had been there only a few days when it was learned that the Nazis were expected.

My Escape from Norway (1940)

BY SIGRID UNDSET

As I had constantly written and spoken against Nazism and had also taken an active part in the work of assisting refugees from central Europe, I was advised to leave town before the Nazis came. A friend had provided a place for me in a motor-car, and that afternoon, with one small suitcase as my entire luggage, I arrived at the People's High School at Hundorp. Here I met some friends who also had fled from the invaders.

We drove north and were in the forest near Dombås together with a few hundred soldiers while the place was being bombed. For two hours we lay flat on our faces in a hole in the snow between two pines. Once, from a neighboring pit, a soldier who said he was from Lillehammer raised his head and reminded me of a dance my boys had had the past Christmas.

Soon it was rumored that the English and Norwegian positions in Tretten Pass were threatened, and we had to flee higher up the valley. The strongest impression from this flight through Norway—all the time behind our retiring lines—was how unspeakably beautiful this country of ours was and how incomparably kind and helpful the people were wherever we met them. . . .

One farm where we stayed during our flight was near Lindsö. A section of parachutists had entrenched themselves in a stone stable and tyrannized the whole neighborhood until the Norwegians got some guns and forced them to surrender. One old housewife thought she recognized one of them. He had come hiking to the farm one day during the previous summer. He had been entertained there with board and room and given money before he went away. It is possible that the housewife was mistaken, but it is certain that many of the "beggar hikers," as we called them—who had traipsed through Norway summer after summer and who had received food and many a time clothing or money from the farmers—had now returned. It is also certain that among the soldiers of the invading army there were many of our *Wienerbarn* or Viennese children—the Germans who, during the lean years after World War I, were taken into Norwegian homes and looked after until they had regained their health and normal childhood.

At this farm we found Norwegian soldiers—boys who had been sent behind the front to rest a few days. Many of them had been fighting in battle after battle. They had retreated, always retreated; but none of those I spoke with was disheartened. They sat in the dark kitchen while we prepared some food for them. Gentle, well-brought-up, nice boys, they were. When they were asked, they talked modestly about their experiences in the campaign. It was a great pity they had not had better equipment and better-trained officers. With only rifles and a few machine guns and a little artillery, it would be impossible in the long run for Norwegians to withstand the German aircraft and armored cars. For all of that, man for man, they were as good as the Germans they had seen, and they hoped they would be allowed to fight again . . . .

At another farm in Langfjord, where we obtained house room for some days, the farmer went about his task of plowing. Aircraft hovered over the region, and sometimes stray shells whined through the air above our heads. We dropped flat on the ground when they came whistling over, but mostly they went into the fjord beyond the houses, and the people refused to be disturbed.

"Did you manage to save any of your chairs and beds?" asked a tiny girl whose home had been burned down. Her parents had saved nothing but their bare lives.

"It is rather hard luck," said the father with grim humor.

One evening we received a message that the English had given up the struggle in south Norway and that the Germans were on their way down the Romsdal. There was nothing for us to do but to flee farther away. The farmer and his wife, who had given us room and food for four days and done their utmost to make us comfortable, refused to accept any payment. The husband shook us warmly by the hand, but his wife embraced us and burst into tears. In other times it is not the nature of Norwegian peasant women to wear their hearts on their sleeves like that, and it was as if her tears first made us realize how dark things looked in Norway.

In one of the outer reaches of the sea, near Hustadvik Cove, we got on board a boat that was to go northward to Bodö. Perhaps, at any rate, that part of Norway was still free. The boat had accommodations for six, and there were thirty-six of us, mostly women and children. One man, a political writer, lay there lame and broken down by gout and sciatica. His young son and daughter were watching their father like guardian angels. There also were soldiers who had fled when they heard about the capitulation of the Norwegian troops. These last intended to make their way northward to the remmant that was still left of our army.

We sailed in the nighttime. In the daytime we lay hidden in harbors between the outermost islands. Day after day the sea lay calm and smooth. Night after night the red evening passed into the aurora. A soldier lent me his sleeping bag, and every night he made it up for me and put me inside it.

We sailed between the white mountains of Nordland and the islands with forms resembling fantastic sculptures. Four hours before we reached Bodö we were told that civilians were seldom allowed to land; but if we liked we might go by another boat back to Mo in Rana. From there it would then be possible to make one's way across country to Sweden.

The last stage of our journey, from Mo across the frontier, was the worst. We started in a lorry. The chauffeur who drove us took us in a tightrope dance up a mountain road, along precipices, in eternal windings and meanderings. We were pitched high up in the air; we slithered to the left and to the right. Sometimes we got stuck in the ice. Then we pushed and heaved and after hours of hard work succeeded in getting the car on the move again.

Thus we did only twelve miles that first night. How it felt for the gouty man to get shaken and knocked about during all these hours is not easy to imagine. At the mountain hut where we spent the night we got the accustomed cordial reception. A houseful of road workers was quartered there, but they turned out to give their berths to us.

The sons of the owner of the hut constructed a stretcher on which the sick man could be carried, and the next afternoon we continued our journey on foot. Then we traveled by motorcar some distance over the same impossible road. At the end we had in front of us several miles of skiing across the mountain to the last farmstead on the Norwegian side of the frontier.

The sick man now had been put in a hay sled. It had been

more than twenty years since I had had skiis on my feet, and, since I found it difficult to keep up with the ski-runners, I also was put on the sled. It was pulled by six young men, and by and by we reached a frontier post. The majority of our company remained there, but I went on with the invalid and his son and daughter. Just as morning dawned over white mountains, we were pulled across a lake, the center of which marked the boundary between Norway and Sweden. The ice was rotten with water, so that the men who pulled the sleigh sometimes sank into it up to their knees and water splashed high around the sleigh.

The first golden sunray was lighting the mountains when we encountered the first Swedish frontier guard who directed us to the nearest military post, but when we got there we found that it was full. A few miles farther on, we were told, we could find shelter in the hut of some road workers who were stationed there.

It was now impossible to use the sleigh, and again the invalid had to be carried on his stretcher. His daughter and I went ahead on foot, and it was five o'clock in the morning when at last the tiny gray hut showed up at the turn of the road. There was a stove in the middle of the floor, but no fire in it, and it was colder inside the hut than outdoors. Along the walls were berths covered with straw and withered leaves, and in one of them lay a man rolled up in a red counterpane. He was sleeping like a stone and did not wake up when we made a fire in the stove to warm the room before the invalid arrived.

The girl and I then sat down on two stools to wait for the stretcher-bearers. When they came, the man in the berth jumped up and stared about with wild blue eyes below a yellow thatch. "Has the war come?" he cried, thinking the stretcher-bearers had come with a wounded man. When we explained the situation he put the coffeepot on the fire and pulled out his store of provisions. We were then invited to a meal of bread and butter, sausage and cheese, coffee and milk.

We had been received hospitably everywhere else but never before with such jolly kindheartedness as was displayed by that Swedish road laborer. After fourteen hours of exertions, we livened up under his infectious joy and goodness.

Later in the day the rest of the company came across the frontier, and then we were taken in charge by the Swedish military. It was strange to get to a hotel again, and here we heard about the German invasion of Holland and Belgium. When I reached Stockholm I received my first word from Norway.

My elder son Anders had been killed in action on April 27. Since then Luxembourg and France have shared the fate of my own Norway and all other countries overrun by the Nazis.

*   *   *

While staying with friends in Stockholm, Mrs. Undset was joined by her surviving son, Hans. They made their way through Russia and Siberia on the Trans-Siberian Railway to Japan. From there they sailed for America, but Hans soon left to rejoin his company, which was being re-formed in Britain. His mother remained an exile in the United States, writing and lecturing, and finding that the friendship of the American people made her anxieties easier to bear until the Nazis were finally driven out of Norway.

Sigrid Undset was in Oslo on June 7, 1945, when King Haakon was welcomed back by cheering crowds. The date, which also marked the fortieth anniversary of Norway's independence, was one of special joy for a people whose freedom had just been restored.

The end of the war also brought liberation to neighboring Denmark. Though King Christian X had surrendered and the country officially was under so-called German "protection," the majority of Danes considered themselves at war. Several underground resistance groups were formed that made life miserable for the invaders. Strikes spread and there were frequent cases of sabotage.

Nor was Christian a mere puppet king, and he had insisted that the Jewish minority not be molested. Since other Danes did not feel inferior to the Jews, they felt no need to persecute them, he said— a pointed remark that infuriated the Nazi overlords. In September,

1943, when rumors spread that the Nazis planned to make mass arrests on the Jewish New Year and deport the unfortunate victims to slave labor camps in Germany, all Denmark was on the alert. Members of the underground hid Jewish friends in fishermen's cottages and in villages near the east coast. In one of the most daring mass rescues in history, nearly all of the 7000 Jewish citizens were transported in small boats across the narrow strait between Denmark and Sweden.

A leader in the Danish resistance movement was the well known author and explorer, Peter Freuchen. He helped many refugees to reach Sweden and himself found sanctuary there before coming to the United States. "The Swedes received us all with open hands and hearts," he said. "We shall never be able to repay their hospitality."

9

Refugees from the Netherlands

It was in Holland, the chief province of the Netherlands, that the Pilgrims found sanctuary before they came to America, and through most of their history the Dutch have been a tolerant people. At one time during the 1840s, a number of dissenters from the Dutch Reformed Church, which had become the state church, objected to the doctrines preached by the ministers in the pay of the government. In protest two Protestant clergymen, Albertus Christian Van Raalte and Henry Peter Scholte, led their entire congregations to America, where they founded the towns of Holland, Michigan, and Pella, Iowa. Still other settlements were started by other dissatisfied Protestants, and also by Catholics, and their enthusiastic reports of the new country encouraged many of their countrymen to emigrate. But it was not until Hitler invaded the Netherlands in 1940 that any Dutch left because they were oppressed.

Queen Wilhelmina fled to London with her Cabinet and set up a government-in-exile. Princess (later Queen) Juliana, with her two small princesses, found refuge in Canada, but she never doubted that her country would be free again.

"Keep your pity for the weak," she said, "for our terrible fate has made us stronger than before."

The future queen's subjects showed the same courage, even the children. What it was like to live in Holland during the first five days of the war was vividly described in the diary of Dirk van der Heide, a twelve-year-old boy who lived with his nine-year-old sister, Keetje, on the outskirts of Rotterdam. Their father, a veterinarian, had left at once to fight the invaders, and the mother, while caring for the wounded at the hospital, had been killed by a bomb.

It was the children's loyal Uncle Pieter who helped them to escape. Later, on the boat taking them to America, Dirk showed his diary to the captain, who suggested that he go over it again and write in more detail about his experiences while they were still fresh in his mind. In 1941 the diary was published under the title *My Sister and I*, from which the following selection has been condensed.

My Sister and I (1940)

BY DIRK van der HEIDE

Sunday, 12th May, 1940. I am writing this in the morning as my sister, Keetje, and I wait for Uncle Pieter. He is taking us to Dordrecht and then to Zeeland if we can get there. I can't believe Mother is dead and that we will never see her again. I cried almost all night, but Keetje still doesn't know. She looks tired, and this morning she vomited again when there was hardly any bombing. That is why Uncle Pieter says we must go away, maybe to England, if we can, or to America. Our uncle in America is name Klaas.

Uncle Pieter left very early and went across the river to try to get all the papers to get to England. I hope he is safe. It is hard to get across the river now and the soldiers are very strict. The fires on the street are not all out yet. The air is still full of smoke. Keetje and I stayed in the air raid shelter across the street. It belongs to my father's friend, the Baron. His face, which is usually red and jolly, looks white and he has great dark circles under his eyes. The radio this morning says the German Nazis have come far into Holland and they are getting most of the bridges that aren't blown up.

No one understands why Holland is losing the war so easily. Uncle Pieter says we didn't have enough antiaircraft guns or planes. We weren't expecting the war from the air or parachutists or tricks like that. Brenda, our *kindermaid* (nurse), has just come in with our traveling bags. We have to wait for Uncle Pieter. Brenda brought Dopfer, Keetje's big doll. Dopfer is very big and Keetje shouldn't try to take him but she wants to.

Later. We are in Dordrecht now and it is late in the afternoon. We are waiting in a café with all our traveling bags. We wanted to go over the Moerdijk bridge by car but the Germans have taken the bridge and we can't go that way. Usually it takes about a half hour on the big new double road to get to Dordrecht. It took us six hours to get here today in Uncle Pieter's car. He has an American car, and it cost about eight thousand guilders. Uncle Pieter is quite gay and rich.

We left home at ten o'clock this morning. I almost cried again and Keetje did cry because Mother didn't come to say goodbye. She couldn't understand it. Brenda kissed us many times. Many people kissed us and said goodbye, some of them I hardly knew. Our house never looked prettier than when we drove away, in spite of the smashed windows and other broken things and the big hole in the street. I hope we don't have to stay away long.

The road out of Rotterdam was full of people going south to get away from the bombing. The electric railways aren't running and there were many people walking and some had bicycles with pieces of baggage strapped onto them. There were all kinds of people, rich and poor. Some of them sat at the roadside and were taking off their shoes and rubbing their sore feet. There were many children. Some of them were being carried and some were being pushed along in baby carriages piled up with food and blankets and canvas bags and things like that.

Uncle Pieter worked his way through the crowd, but he went slowly and carefully. It was a bright sunny day with just a few clouds. Every day since the war it has been sunny. It seems awful to have this all happen just when we were getting ready for a nice summer. The meadows were full of spring flowers of many kinds, but in the middle of many meadows there were Dutch soldiers with machine guns and antiaircraft guns.

About three o'clock some Nazi planes came over. Five of them dived down toward the road until we thought they were falling and then they shot at us with machine guns. We all got under the car and many people crawled in beside us. Other people threw themselves on the ground and dived into the roadside ditches for protection. The planes kept going back and forth above us very low and loud.

There was great confusion. Many children were crying. About fifty people were wounded and many were killed. It made me sick. Uncle Pieter helped all the wounded that he could and then we hurried away.

When we got near Dordrecht we were told not to go into the city but to go around it as there was fighting in the center of the city. We left the main road, and just as we turned off we saw two small children sitting by the side of the road. They looked lost and unhappy. The girl was about as tall as Keetje and with dimples like Keetje's. The boy was much younger, with yellow curls. Uncle Pieter stopped and spoke very gently. He asked where their parents were. They said they didn't know. They thought they were killed. Uncle Pieter asked them where they were going and they didn't say anything, just looked at him. When he asked where they had spent the night they said they didn't know and then said somewhere on the road.

Uncle Pieter sighed and shook his head and said the car was full but we would have to make it fuller. In the car they held hands all the time and looked straight ahead. Uncle Pieter said they were like two lost birds.

We had a hard time in Dordrecht. Uncle Pieter and Keetje and I and the boy and girl went over to a little café. The door was locked. He pounded hard and finally a man let us in. He said he kept the door locked because of the parachutists who might come down any time. Uncle Pieter put some money in his hand and said, "Give these children something to eat and don't let them out of your sight until I get back. I'm going to find out if there are any boats for Vlissingen." Vlissingen is the place to get boats for England.

Uncle Pieter was gone a long time and when he came back he looked pleased and happy. "Late tonight we can get over to Vlissingen," he said. The girl and boy we picked up on the road were still eating. Uncle Pieter found out they were from right here in Dordrecht and their house had been bombed the night before. They had crawled out of the ruins and run away. They were so frightened they had stayed all night. Uncle Pieter gave the café-keeper some money and told him to take care of the children until he found someone who knew them. The café-keeper said he would but he didn't want any money for doing a thing like that. Uncle Pieter shook hands with him and said he was a good man and God would bless him.

All the time we could hear the guns in the distance. At ten o'clock Uncle Pieter said it was time to go. He gave the car to the café-keeper and told him to guard it well for he didn't know how many days it would be until he got back.

We took our things out and walked up the street in the dark. The farther we went the more people we passed in the darkness. When we got to the place where the boat was, there were hundreds of people trying to get onto the boat.

13th May. It took us many hours to get to Vlissingen. The boat sailed without lights. All the time we kept thinking of our friends at home and wondering if the bombs were falling, and of course about Father. It doesn't seem right that we should be so safe when they are still there where the bombs are. I told Uncle Pieter this and he said we were not safe yet.

I found out later why. Dordrecht is on a big river or canal and when it ends and goes to the sea we had to pass the Moerdijk bridge. The Nazis were there but I was asleep and did not know this until later.

Uncle Pieter says we are not running away, we are just doing the sensible thing for Keetje's sake. He didn't say anything about me and I was glad because I had been trying all day to prove I was not just a big baby the way I had been the night before when he told me about Mother. In Vlissingen we waited for a boat and Uncle Pieter got places for us in spite of all the other refugees. We are going to England tomorrow night.

14th May. The boat has started and I wish I could go out on deck. But this is not permitted. It is late at night. There are no lights on the outside of the boat. Inside there is some light but the portholes are covered. We can hardly see a thing through the cabin windows. There is not a single light in Vlissingen because of the bombers. There are no beds for us and we have to sit up but Uncle Pieter has taken Keetje in his arms and she is asleep now.

Later. The boat has been tossing around a great deal. I asked Uncle Pieter how long it will take to get to England. He says a good while because we have to go back and forth zigzag to get through the mine fields in the water. I'm glad we're going to England, and I hope the Nazis don't come there the way they did in Holland.

I forgot to say how nice Keetje was before we left Dordrecht. She gave her big doll, Dopfer, to the little girl. Keetje was nice to do this. I pray God will keep our father safe. We could not bear to lose Father after what happened to Mother. Uncle Pieter is very good to take care of us while Father is away fighting the Nazis.

15th May. We have been in England all morning. We landed at a place called Harwich. Everyone cheered and sang when we came into the harbor safely. We took the train to London and went to a place in the station where refugees have to go. There were many English people there to give us breakfast and to help us. They were all very cheerful and smiling.

Some of the refugees looked ill and very unhappy and lost.

There were children there without any parents or relatives or friends. Some of the children were French and Belgian. There were several English doctors there and some of them spoke Dutch. They were helping to fix wounded people. Uncle Pieter has taken us to a hotel near the station. I am writing this in the hotel. Uncle Pieter says most of the Dutch and Belgian and French refugees are going to the country away from London so that if the bombs come again they will be safe. They will go to Ireland and Yorkshire and the Isle of Man and places like that where I have never been.

Uncle Pieter has gone away to send a cable to our Uncle Klaas in America and to see the American Consul. Maybe we will go to America later, he says. If we do he is not going to go with us. He is going back to Holland to tell Father where we are. No one can send a cable to Holland now. It is fine to be in this country where it is so quiet and peaceful the way home was.

Later. Uncle Pieter came in with an English newspaper. I can read some of it easily. A funny thing happened. Queen Wilhelmina took a boat from Zeeland yesterday too. It is all written about in the English paper. The English king met her at Liverpool Street station and kissed her on both cheeks. The queen was probably very glad to see him but I didn't know she knew the English king well enough to let him kiss her on both cheeks. Crown Princess Juliana was there too, the paper says, and also Prince Bernhard and the Princess Beatrix who is two years old and Princess Irene who is just a baby. There is a picture of them all in the paper. Princess Juliana is carrying Irene in her arms and Prince Bernhard and a nurse are carrying a box that the paper says is a gas-proof box for babies. It looks more like a puppy box than anything else. Little Beatrix must be in the box.

Things must be very bad with our government if the queen has come to England. Uncle Pieter says the Dutch government has moved from The Hague to London, the Cabinet and all.

Later. Uncle Pieter has just come back with terrible news. Holland has surrendered to the Germans. It is all in the newspapers. Uncle Pieter is almost crying. He says the fall of Holland threatens England and we must go to America if we can get a boat. I asked Uncle Pieter if we couldn't go home now that the war is over and he said never, never could we go back there while the Nazis were there. He says it is worse than death for Hollanders to live as slaves. I hope the Nazis don't make a slave out of Father. I don't think they could. Father gets very angry and he would not stand for it.

1st July. We have been in England many weeks. Now we are in Liverpool waiting for a boat to America. Uncle Pieter has heard from Uncle Klaas in America and he wants Keetje and me to come. Uncle Klaas had to cable the American Consul and his bankers in America had to do the same thing. Uncle Pieter had to get visas and things and all kinds of papers and pay a great deal of money, I think.

We are having much fun in England but we miss Holland. Keetje was ill for a week in the hotel in London. A doctor came to see her and said she was nervous. He gave her some medicine. He was very kind. He wouldn't let Uncle Pieter pay him anything. He said it was his pleasure and his gift to gallant Holland. Uncle Pieter argued with him but the kind doctor said no. Uncle Pieter says the English are just that way and good enough people when you know them.

Dear Uncle Pieter. He is so sad about Holland and so good to us. In London he took us everywhere. The policemen—bobbies, they are called!—are very funny and big and polite. We asked them many questions on walks when we got lost. All over London there are many things for war. There are many trenches everywhere and sandbags too.

There are big black and white posters everywhere with ARP printed on them. This means Air Raid Precautions. People all carry gas masks and we have them now. They were fitted on us by a nice woman in London. The gas masks have long snouts and look as funny as the Dutch ones. Uncle Pieter put his on yesterday for the first time and looked at himself. He said he looked no better with it than without it. I laughed and he laughed too. I was glad to see him laugh for he has been so sad. When he reads the newspapers about the war he gets sadder and sadder. When Belgium fell he was almost sick.

There are no street lights in England after dark. We have only been out once late at night. We were in a taxi with Uncle Pieter coming home from the Mickey Mouse cinema. There are no crossing lights except little shaded crosses no bigger than a button. It is very exciting going along in the dark.

My English is improving. I practice it on the chambermaid. So does Keetje. Keetje gets more practice than I do because everyone stops to talk with her. She is very cute-looking in the new sailor hat Uncle Pieter bought her. We are in Liverpool now. Liverpool is not so big as London. It has many boats, though, and we like to go down to the wharves because they remind us of dear Holland. We are staying at a big hotel named the Adelphi. Everything in it is big. The bathtub is almost big enough to swim in, and Keetje tried it and took a few strokes. The dining room is big too.

Uncle Pieter has just come in with news. He has just had news from the ticket office that we have a passage and will leave sometime soon. He says he cannot go to see us off as it is against the rules because of the war. The ticket man is sending someone for us. I asked him the name of the boat and he said he didn't know that either because the ticket office couldn't let any secrets out because of the Nazis.

I must stop writing now and help Keetje and Uncle Pieter pack. Goodbye, England. We have to leave you just as we were beginning to love you. I suppose we will have to get used to having new homes since we can't go back to our own dear home in Holland.

3rd July. We are on the boat now. We sailed yesterday sometime after dark. It was hard to leave Uncle Pieter. He kissed us many times and hugged us hard. He cried when we left him. He is the only man I ever saw cry. He is going to let us know about Father if he gets back to Holland. Uncle Klaas will meet us in New York. We are on a big boat and there are so many people going away because of the war that some of them have to sleep in bunks in the smoking rooms and halls.

Everything is very strict on this English boat. Before we sailed a sailor told us what we could do and what we couldn't. We are not allowed on deck after the trumpet sounds in the evening. All the portholes are covered with thick cloths to blot out the light. The ship doesn't even have lights on it to see by at night because of the submarines. The English sailor said no one could smoke on deck at night. A lighted cigarette can be seen two miles at sea, he says. If anyone disobeys he will be severely punished and put in a room and locked up for the rest of the trip.

There are double doors at the dining saloon and we go in on the side so the lights don't show. There are many ships sailing beside us. We counted twenty. Six carry passengers and the rest are going along to keep the submarines away. There are topedo boats, warships, and one airplane carrier. They keep very near us all the time and we weave back and forth. The boats are all painted gray so they will be hard to see in the water. Everyone is afraid of the German submarines. The English captain says for me not to worry because anyone who was born around as much water as we have in Holland just couldn't be drowned. He is a nice man and is always making jokes.

I have never been on such a big boat. This one is like the Adelphi Hotel in Liverpool, only it wobbles. A man was caught smoking a cigarette today and put into a room and locked up just as the sailor said he would be.

28th September. I have not written in my diary for so long. Not since I got to America. Uncle Klaas and Aunt Helen met us. Aunt Helen is an American with long red fingernails and a very pretty face. Our boat came in to New York at night on

the tenth day after we left England. We came slowly because
our boat had to take a longer way because of the war. We
stayed all night in the harbor. We thought New York looked
very exciting in the distance. There were so many lights and
they were all on. All during the time we were in England there
had never been any lights at night in the streets. It looked fine
to see so many all going at once with so many colors.

Uncle Klaas took us off the boat the next morning, and when
we got through the customs we drove to Uncle Klaas's apartment at Morningside Heights. The streets were very exciting.
I remember particularly when we crossed one and Uncle Klaas
said, "This is Broadway. I came over here just to show you."
Uncle Klaas and Aunt Helen have a beautiful apartment that
is near the river. Maybe he took it because he is Dutch and
always wants to be near some water.

We have been in America several weeks now. Keetje and I
go to a private school. We like it very much although it was
strange at first. I am learning to play football and other sports.
Keetje likes the movies and the drugstore sodas best. Keetje
seems very happy. Sometimes I think she has forgotten about
Mother entirely. But I haven't. Everyone is very kind to us and
I have been made a monitor at school. My English has improved and I have learned many new words that I never heard
in England and some not in my dictionary.

Several letters have come from England from Uncle Pieter.
He has not been able to get back to Holland. He is working for
the English now and is a volunteer fire warden. Uncle Pieter
says he misses us. He has had one letter from Father and we
have had one. Father is safe and back in Rotterdam. The letter
we got from him had a Swiss stamp. It must not have been seen
by the Nazis, Uncle Klass says.

Father tells about what Holland is like now. There is not
much food. No taxis are running. None of the Dutch can listen
to the radio to anything but Spanish, Italian, and German pro-
grams without being fined and two years in prison. People

have to stay home after ten o'clock at night. The food is getting worse and worse. Father wants to come to America. I wish he could and so does Keetje. We write to him often but we don't know whether he gets our letters. I will be so glad when the war is over.

Keetje and I are happy here and everything would be perfect if Father and Uncle Pieter were here. I haven't had very good marks at school. The doctor says I am nervous and can't concentrate very well yet because of the bombing but that I will be all right later. The American doctor was just like the English one Uncle Pieter had for Keetje. He wouldn't charge any money for taking care of me. He said, "This is on me," which is slang but very kind.

I know I am nervous sometimes. When airplanes go over I want to run and hide. One night when it was raining I woke up and heard the rain on the glass and was frightened. I thought I was back in Holland and that what was striking the windows were pieces of bombs.

That is why Uncle Klaas doesn't like it when people ask me about the war. I heard him tell Aunt Helen that he wanted Keetje and me to forget about the war. But I know I'll never forget about it anyway, or how Mother died. I won't forget America either. It is a good country that has made us feel welcome. Keetje is looking over my shoulder as I write this and says, "Why don't you say it's swell?" That's an American word.

I know one reason why I'll always love America. It's because of something that happened on the boat trip here. When we were one day away from New York all the battleships and boats that had brought us over so safely turned around and went back toward England. We were very frightened. Then someone started yelling and pointing at the sky. There was a big zeppelin over us. It said "United States Naval Patrol Number 14" in big letters. We all yelled and cheered. I won't ever forget that Number 14 and the nice safe way it made us feel. The zeppelin followed us and watched over us all the rest of the way to America.

People have been watching over us ever since and there haven't been any bombings. Not one. And that is why Keetje and I are happy now.

10

Refugees from Poland

A refugee who helped to ensure the success of the American Revolution was an astute young businessman named Haym Salomon. Though of Portuguese Jewish descent, he had been born in Poland, which through the years has been victimized again and again by stronger neighbors. The first partition of Polish territory took place in 1772, when the weak government was forced to cede vast areas to Russia, Austria, and Prussia. Young Salomon, because he took part in an uprising, was faced with prison and fled, first to New York and later to Philadelphia.

In this city where the Continental Congress was meeting, he became a successful broker. He was of much help to Robert Morris, merchant and financier, whose task was to raise the funds needed to keep an army in the field. Like Morris, Salomon used his personal credit to negotiate loans for the shaky new government. He also made personal loans, without much expectation of repayment, to members of the Continental Congress. Without this help a number of them—among them James Madison, who later became President —could not have afforded to serve. Because of Salomon's efforts to help "the cause," as he always referred to the American struggle, he died poor. But he lived long enough to see the United States win its independence.

Among the Polish-American soldiers dedicated to the cause of freedom was Count Casimir Pulaski, who was commissioned a brigadier general in the Continental Army and mortally wounded in battle two years later. One of the most popular officers from abroad, Thaddeus Kosciusko, was a skillful engineer who rendered great

101

service by constructing the first fortifications at West Point. After his return to Poland, he was the leader in unsuccessful uprisings of his people to try to prevent the second and third partitions of their country.

After the third partition, Poland ceased to exist as a nation on the maps of Europe, but not in the hearts of Polish patriots. Several revolts ended in failure and sent more refugees to America. Young men came to avoid military service in the armies of their conquerors. Jews came to avoid religious persecution. The bright side of the coin was that many of the newcomers enriched their adopted country with their talents, their labor, and their loyalty.

One Pole, as much admired in America as in his own country, was the world-famous pianist Ignace Jan Paderewski. He frequently gave concerts in the United States, which during World War I earned large sums for Polish relief. He successfully pleaded his country's cause with President Woodrow Wilson, who insisted in the peace negotiations on the establishment of an independent Poland. As a result of the Allied victory, the Polish Republic was proclaimed, with Paderewski as its first premier.

Thirty years later, however, he was to witness another tragic act in the drama of Poland's history. In September, 1939, the military forces of Nazi Germany, without any declaration of war, quickly overran the country—an act of aggression that began World War II. The Nazis were finally driven out by the forces of the Soviet Union, which by 1945 was in control of most of Eastern Europe. In a conference with American and British leaders, Joseph Stalin, the Soviet premier, agreed that free elections were to be held in Poland and the people permitted to vote on the kind of government they preferred. This agreement was never kept, and Poland became a Communist state.

What life was like under the Nazis has been vividly described by Jan Karski, who became a professor of political science in America. As a young man in Poland he had joined the Underground, determined as were the other members of the resistance movement to make it as difficult as possible for the Nazi invaders. Imprisonment and torture by the Gestapo, the secret police, failed to break his spirit, and when he was transferred from one prison hospital to another it seemed an almost incredible piece of good fortune to find himself in a familiar town, where he had once worked with other members of the Underground. The following account is taken from his book *The Story of a Secret State*.

Rescue (1944)

BY JAN KARSKI

The guards flanking me, I tottered up the stairs. I was genuinely sick and weak, but I exaggerated my condition. They were obliged to carry me to the second floor, where they dumped me unceremoniously on a bed.

When the guards had left, I propped myself up on one elbow and studied my roommates. There were five of them, all old, ranging in age, it appeared to me, from seventy to eighty. What were the Nazis up to? I wondered. Perhaps, I reflected, they wanted to make me feel overconfident and betray myself. Then it occured to me that I might have been taken to this town especially to lure my friends and colleagues into the open. But it did not seem possible that they could know my connections with this place. My mind gnawed anxiously at this problem, but I could reach no definite conclusion.

The muttering of these old men ceased abruptly. I had been in a hospital long enough to know that this signaled the entrance of the Gestapo. I closed my eyes and writhed feebly on the bed. Alongside my bed, a man and a woman were conversing in Polish, and I judged them to be a doctor and a nurse. The guard must have been hovering nearby for the doctor addressed him curtly.

"Isn't it your duty to guard the room from the corridor? You won't do any good by crowding me."

The guard did not answer and walked away heavily, his footsteps resounding like a cannonade in the oppressive silence.

The doctor bent over me to examine and dress my wounds.

As he unwound the clotted and filthy bandages, he fired questions at me in a rapid, anxious whisper.

"Where did they arrest you? May I help you? Shall I let someone know about you?"

The circumstances were not such as to arouse my trust easily. I suspected a trick and answered in aggrieved and injured tones, "I have no one to send messages to."

"Don't be afraid," he whispered. "I am not a provocateur. The entire staff—doctors, nurses, and attendants—is all Polish and there is not a single traitor or renegade among us."

I opened my eyes and stared intently at him. He was extremely young for a doctor. His guileless countenance made me feel like opening my heart in a burst of confidence, but the prudence and caution that had become second nature by this time checked my impulse. I said nothing.

The following morning, a sister (all the nurses were nuns from a nearby convent) entered my ward, nodded at me, and without a word inserted a thermometer between my lips. She watched me impassively, then removed the thermometer and read it. I gazed anxiously at the mercury. It had stopped at 100 degrees. She took the chart in her hand, gravely entered a figure of 103 degrees, and then left the ward. She returned quickly with an elderly man who introduced himself as the head physician. He raised his voice and addressed me harshly.

"Look here, young man," he snapped. "You are very sick, but we can only give you proper medical treatment. If you want to live you must rest and avoid anxiety. If you don't follow my advice"—he shrugged callously—"we can always use this bed for our townsfolk. Now lie quietly and let me examine you."

He turned to the nurse and ordered her to remove a tray and bring some ointments and bandages. As she left the room, she stumbled against the guard, scattering the contents of the tray on the floor. He hastened to help her pick them up. While they were engaged in groping about on the floor, the doctor whispered to me. "Courage—as soon as I leave, begin moaning and whining. Shout that you are going to die and that you wish to go to confession."

When the nurse returned, he issued crisp, peremptory instructions to her.

"Change his dressings every two hours and see that he doesn't get out of bed."

As he turned on his heel, he barked to me, "As for you, if you want to live, follow instructions."

After the nurse changed my bandages, I began to twist about, gradually working up to a series of frenzied, convulsive movements accompanied by loud moans.

I wailed loudly, "I am going to die—to die, do you hear? I want to be confessed. Please, Sister, please, speak to the doctor. You are a good Catholic. Don't let me die a sinner."

She glanced at me stonily and walked over to consult the young Gestapo man. His face was blankly devoid of either intelligence or stupidity, sympathy or cruelty. Sitting, his posture was rigid and unyielding. He never even allowed himself the luxury of tilting his chair. He seemed to regard himself as the incarnation of Nazi discipline and prestige. When the sister addressed him, he snapped to attention and stiffly nodded his agreement.

She returned with the head physician, who eyed me with annoyance.

"Can't you be a man? If you have determined to die, there is nothing we can do about it. Bring him a wheelchair, please, Sister."

I continued to moan and whine. The doctor shouted at me, "Enough of your moans! You are getting your way. You are going to be confessed."

A wheelchair was brought in. The nurse tucked me into a bathrobe and helped me into it. She wheeled me out of the room, the Nazi guard marching behind us as if he were on military parade.

I made my confession to an old, kindly priest. At the conclusion, he placed his hands on my shoulders and said in consolation, "Do not be afraid, boy. Maintain your faith in God. We are all aware of your suffering for our beloved Poland. Everyone in this hospital is anxious to help you."

My confession left me with a feeling of tranquillity and peace. It did not endure very long, for during the next few days I had to concentrate on the task of making myself appear deathly ill, and I actually became a very sick man. Chills and feverish spells alternated and my temperature was always abnormal.

Consequently I had been granted a concession by the hospital authorities. I was permitted to be brought into the chapel daily. One day while I was praying in the chapel, the sister who brought me in the wheelchair knelt down beside me. I studied her face with its courageous, determined lines and decided to risk everything. I knew that I could not speak to her while there were other people in the chapel, so I asked if she would mind waiting for me to finish praying. She said she would wait. While I sat there I could hear the faint click of the rosary slipping between her fingers. The coolness and quiet of the chapel with its familiar, faintly exotic smell of incense, her calm firmness, gave me reassurance. I felt certain I could trust her. Finally we were alone. I leaned over to whisper to her.

"Sister, I know you are a good woman. But it is important for me to know if you are a good Pole."

She looked me full in the face for a moment and, continuing to tell her rosary, said simply, "I love Poland."

But it was not necessary for her to tell me. I had seen her eyes. I spoke rapidly, in a low voice.

"I want to ask you to do something. But before I tell you what it is, I must tell you that it may be dangerous for you. You are free to refuse, of course."

"Tell me what you want. If I can do it, I will."

"Thank you," I said fervently. "I knew you would say that.

Here is what I would like you to do. There is a family in this town by the name of————. They have a daughter, Stefi. Find her and tell her what has happened to me. Tell her Witold sent you." I gave her the address. "Witold" was my pseudonym in the Underground.

"Today," she said quietly.

After I had made this request, I felt a great burden slip from my mind. Not that I expected much to materialize from it, but at least it lightened the feeling of being alone in a hostile world. When I saw the sister again, I looked at her with questioning eyes.

She whispered, "In a few days, you will be visited by a nun from a convent nearby."

"A nun? Why should a nun visit me?"

"I don't know. I was told to give you this message."

I was on tenterhooks for the next two days. I realized that if my friends were going to the length of sending a person as innocuous in appearance as a nun to visit me, it meant that some definite plan was already afoot. The third day after this conversation, shortly after noon, the nun arrived. I could hear the rasping breathing and snoring of the old men as they slept in the drowsy afternoon sunshine that filtered into the dingy ward. She moved toward me as if on tiptoe, approaching my bed with short, hesitant steps.

There was a vague familiarity about her delicate, pale face, but I could not place her as I was peeping with one eye, not daring to allow myself a closer scrutiny till she reached the bed. Then recognition was quickly kindled in an instant of excitement and fear. It was the sister of the guide who had been apprehended with me by the Gestapo.

Her voice was girlish but firm as she introduced herself.

"I am a nun from a nearby convent. The German authorities have permitted us to bring cigarettes and food to the prisoners. Is there anything you need?"

I simulated great weakness and murmured inaudibly so that

she would have to stoop to hear me. She understood this maneuver and said in a voice distinct enough to be heard by the
guard, "I am sorry, I can't hear you."

Then, stooping over, she whispered, "Word has been sent to
your superiors. Be patient."

I had learned the technique of speaking without moving my
lips. "What happened to your brother?" I asked her, keeping
an eye on the guard. Tears welled up in her eyes.

"We haven't heard from him."

It was no use attempting to console her with hypocrisies.
Losses of that kind cannot be mitigated by cheerful, empty
phrases.

"I want you to tell them that I must have some poison. I am
sure the Gestapo have brought me here to make me give away
the Underground in this vicinity. I can't stand any more torture."

"I understand. Take good care of yourself. I will return in a
few days."

The period till she returned was one of endless suspense. It
was like being thirsty and seeing water at a distance which was
too great to be reached. Beyond the hospital walls, plans were
being formulated for my rescue, and I could almost taste liberty and freedom in the offing. It was maddening to be in bed,
waiting.

When she finally returned, she brought me fruit and cigarettes and placed them on the shelf next to my bed. Again we
employed the stratagems devised during her first visit. I muttered. She stooped, cupping her hand to her ear. Then we
would whisper, hurriedly, our words tumbling over each other
in our desire to crowd as much information as possible into a
short moment.

"They know everything," she whispered. "You have been
awarded the Cross of Valor." She pretended to smooth my
pillow and whispered without looking at me, "I have just put
a cyanide pill under your pillow. It kills quickly. I implore you,

don't use it unless you are absolutely sure the worst has come."

I looked at her gratefully.

After her departure, I felt a surge of courage and determination. I was now armed against the worst contingencies. The poison gave me a sense of luxury, a feeling that I had a magic talisman against the eventualities which I had dreaded most—torture and the possibility that I might crack and betray the organization. As soon as I could I went to the lavatory and carefully hid the tiny capsule. She had left me a piece of flesh-colored adhesive for the purpose, the hiding place being the customary one for prisoners—the perineum.

So great was this feeling of security that it served even to quell my disappointment at the fact that the nun had given no intimation of a plan for my escape. Not wishing to appear querulous or demanding, I had stifled the questions that had been on the tip of my tongue all during her visit. However, events soon began to move with a much greater rapidity than I had anticipated.

That evening the young doctor came to give me what I presumed was merely a routine examination. When he was through, he peered quizzically at my face as if trying to read in it my chances for recovery. Then in a normal, semihumorous tone that left me aghast at his seeming imprudence, he drawled, "Well, you are going to be set free tonight."

I started as though I had been stung. Sitting bolt upright, I hissed indignantly, "Are you mad? Don't talk so loud! The guard will hear you. He has left only for a moment—probably to get water or something. For heaven's sake, be careful."

He chuckled good-humoredly. "Don't worry. We have bribed him. He won't come back while I am here. Now listen carefully. Everything has been arranged. At midnight, I will pass this room and light a cigarette. That is your cue to go to the first floor. On one of the window sills you will find a rose. Jump from that sill. Men will be stationed below." He paused a moment. "Is everything clear?"

My heart pounded like a trip-hammer.

"Yes, yes, I understand perfectly." I repeated his directions. He grinned and patted me on the shoulder.

"Relax," he said, "and don't worry. Good luck!"

He could not have given me advice more impossible to follow. A thousand doubts rose to my mind. Most of my time I spent in scrutinizing the guard who returned to his post shortly afterward. Could he have merely pretended to accept the bribe in order to set a trap for my comrades? He had appeared to be so thoroughly indoctrinated with the Nazi code. I felt reassured when he turned toward me. There was a faint smirk of greed and self-satisfaction upon his lips, which I interpreted to mean that he was content with his pickings and impatient to begin indulging himself in the wealth he had been promised.

Of course, he did not realize that the money he would receive, the forged papers that he had indubitably been provided with, did not mean that a life of ease was within his grasp. The Underground had bribed hundreds like him before and then had turned the tables by mercilessly "exploiting" them, as it was termed in underground language, forcing them to cooperate in other schemes by holding over their heads the constant threat of exposure to the Gestapo.

Some time before midnight the guard pretended to drop off into a deep sleep. His head on his chest, he emitted stentorian snores. Precisely as the church clock tolled the hour of midnight, the figure of the doctor appeared in the doorway. He drew a cigarette from his pocket, lit it with slow, conspicuous gestures, and moved on. I gave the ward a cursory inspection. An encouraging medley of snores, breathing, and sleepy groans issued from all sides. I slid out of bed, took off my hospital pajamas, and stuffed them under the cover. I transferred the cyanide pill to my hand, ready to swallow it in case of sudden danger. Completely naked, I padded down to the first floor.

Slightly bewildered, I studied the dimly lit corridor. My sense of direction had vanished momentarily and, since there were two similar staircases, I could not tell which was the front or the back of the hospital. In this strange dilemma, I felt a draft of cold air on my back. I reasoned that a window had been left open for me, as whoever had engineered the scheme would probably realize that I would be unable to open one unaided.

I headed in the direction of the open window. My heart leaped with exultation as I saw the rose, which had been blown from the sill to the floor. I stared for a moment at the inky blackness below and then, taking a deep, decisive breath, I clambered to the sill and jumped without further ado, still clutching the little pill.

As I hit the ground and began to totter, a pair of strong arms caught and held me erect. The suddenness of the embrace frightened me, and for a moment I thought I was in the hands of the Gestapo. My relief was immense when someone slipped a coat over me, handed me a pair of trousers and rapped out commandingly, "Hurry, we haven't a moment to lose. Run like the devil."

Both of my rescuers were barefooted. We sped across the lawn until we reached a fence. I had not the faintest idea who my rescuers were or to what underground organization they belonged. We paused at the fence, panting from the sprint.

One of them spoke. "It will be impossible for you to get over the fence without help. This is what we will do. I'll climb over first. Then our friend will bend down. You get on his back, climb on the fence, and jump. I'll catch you."

He scrambled neatly over the fence. We performed the operation as he had directed. Then the other member came over. When we were all together, we continued to run, over a muddy field, across two paved roads toward a row of protecting trees. My bare feet began to smart with pain, my ribs ached, and I felt a burning, choking sensation in my lungs each time I inhaled. Finally I stumbled, pitched forward, and collapsed on the ground, gasping for breath.

"I can't make it," I gasped. "I am sorry to cause you so much trouble but I must have some rest."

They did not answer me. One of the men, an unusually tall, burly individual, reached down and flung me over his shoulder as though I had been a bundle of old clothes. I must have lost a great deal of weight for he carried me, without the slightest stagger, into the woods.

When we were well within the comforting darkness, one of the men gave an audible sigh of relief.

"I guess we can rest here a bit," he suggested to the man on whose shoulder I hung limply.

The latter deposited me on a mound of earth under a tree. I leaned back against the tree, trying to recover my breath and bearings. They lit cigarettes and offered me one, which I waved away speechlessly. After a few puffs, they held a brief monosyllabic conversation, stood up, and threw away the butts, ready to resume the trek.

"Do you think you can walk yet?" the tall, burly one asked me.

"I-I don't think so. Have we far to go?"

Without answering, he bent down again and flipped me over his shoulder. They walked at a steady methodical pace for about fifteen minutes and then emerged from the woods onto what looked like a broad, open field. The moon, which had been obscured by clouds, broke through, illumining a river so that I saw the faint silvery glimmer of water before us. The two men stopped and my carrier set me on my feet. The other placed his fingers in his mouth and emitted a thin, piercing whistle.

From behind the bushes to our right, two men stepped forward—two of the hardiest, toughest-looking individuals I have ever encountered. One of them held a revolver in his hand and the other a long knife which glinted evilly in the moonlight.

They held a brief, inaudible conference with my rescuers. Then the husky one, whom I judged to be the leader of the expedition, beckoned me to follow him along the reedy, marshy ground by the side of the river. The five of us churned through the slush until a man who had apparently been lying prone in the reeds jumped up, his face split in a wide grin.

"Good evening, gentlemen," he greeted us.

I recognized him immediately. His name was Staszek Rosa. I had first met him in Cracow, and although I knew he was well-informed about the Underground, I was puzzled by his flippancy and apparent carelessness. I had never suspected him of being so deep in organization work. For this reason, I was surprised to see him and even more astonished to realize that this devil-may-care attitude was a convenient cloak to hide the courage and determination necessary for the important work he was doing.

He directed his attentions to me by slapping my shoulder good-humoredly. "Congratulations, Jan, on your divorce from the Gestapo. I bet that was one wedding you didn't care for, eh?"

"No, I can't say that I enjoyed it much. Where do we go from here?"

"Follow me, you heroes," he chirped. He walked a few paces, bent over, waved his hands in the air like a magician on a stage, and then proceeded to draw out a canoe which had been cleverly concealed in the thick underbrush.

"Presto, there it is," he announced when the task was finished.

We boarded the canoe, giving the paddle to the man who had carried me. We headed for the opposite bank of the river against a heavy current. The canoe rocked violently, tilting out of the water at a dangerous angle. At one point, it slanted so far over on its side that I lost my balance and plunged into the water. The big fellow put down his paddle, steadied the canoe, and hauled me back as though I had been a fish.

We struggled against the tricky tide for more than an hour, while I lay prone on the bottom of the canoe, soaked to the skin, shivering and trying to control my chattering teeth. When we reached the shore, we clambered out, wading in a couple of inches of water, and then they concealed the canoe again. On shore I swung my arms and stamped up and down, trying to restore a little warmth to my benumbed body.

When the canoe was concealed, we began talking, Staszek Rosa leading the way.

"Well," he said, "it won't be long before you are in your new home."

We cut through a dense wood, then across a field of wheat, and finally, after what seemed to me an extremely circuitous route, stopped in front of a barn.

"The end of the line. All off!" my humorous friend announced.

We entered the barn. The warmth, the fresh odor of the hay, were overwhelmingly soothing to my fatigued senses.

"We must leave you here," he said. "Your host will pay his respects tomorrow. He will see to it that you are well hidden for a while. You will be contacted as soon as the Gestapo chase slackens off."

I began to express my gratitude for the dangerous task they had undertaken on my behalf. Rosa cut me off, a faint, derisive smile on his thin lips. "Don't be too grateful to us. We had two orders about you. The first was to do everything in our power to help you escape. The second was to shoot you if we failed. You were lucky. . . ."

I gaped at him in dumbfounded amazement.

"Pleasant dreams." He chuckled and turned to leave with the others. After they bade me farewell, I climbed up into the loft and sank wearily into the soft hay. I was a free man again.

*   *   *

Later, Jan Karski left Poland, traveling through wartime France and then through Spain, where he sailed for England. After conferring with the leaders of the Polish government-in-exile in London, he came to the United States to report to President Franklin D. Roosevelt about conditions he had observed in the occupied countries. The President impressed him as a man whose "interests embraced not merely his own country but all humanity."

After leaving the White House, Dr. Karski walked across the street to Lafayette Park, where he looked up at the statue of Kosciusko. He thought of the dangerous days of toil in the Underground. He felt fatigued.

"It was not, however, an ordinary fatigue," he said, "but more the satisfied weariness of the workman who has just completed his job with the last blow of his hammer or an artist who signs his name under the completed picture."

I I

Escapees from the U.S.S.R.

The Russian Revolution of November, 1917, which sent a million and a half refugees fleeing for their lives, had been preceded by an earlier revolution in March of that same year. Czar Nicholas II had been forced to abdicate, and Alexander Kerensky became head of a provisional government which many Russians hoped would bring about desperately needed changes. This was the opinion of Julia Grant, a native American who had been born in the White House while her grandfather, Ulysses S. Grant, was President. In 1899 she had married Count Cantacuzene and lived for the next eighteen years in Russia.

"As I saw the revolution preparing," she wrote after her return to her native land, "I joined most heartily in the feelings of my adopted people. The majority of the Emperor's court felt as I did and thought reform absolutely necessary. The army officers (whether aristocrats or bourgeois) had long since wished for the reign of better principles, and my husband was in this heartily with them. . . . The members of Parliament had cried out long since, demanding new laws and responsible ministers. . . . Those who lived through March and April, 1917, will never forget the intense desire to make good in the new situation. . . . Then came the birth of a new thing in politics."

That new thing was Bolshevism, an extreme and radical form of socialism. Two Russians, Vladimir Lenin and Leon Trotzky, who had studied the Communist teachings of Karl Marx, returned from exile and established a new kind of dictatorship under soviets (committees or councils) of peasants, workingmen, and sol-

116

diers. Kerensky was driven from office and forced to flee. The Czar and his family were murdered. Peasants and discontented city workers, who had long been starved and abused, were lured by promises of "a worker's paradise" and took part in the bloody revolution that followed. Too late they realized that the Bolshevik slogan, "Peace, bread, and land," could not be fulfilled overnight.

After the Russian Revolution, all soviets, or local councils, were subservient to the Supreme Soviet, with offices in the Kremlin, an ancient fortress in Moscow, the capital. The soviets were dominated by the Communist Party, though its membership included little more than 1 percent of the total population. As premier, Lenin controlled the destinies of the millions of Russians, and his death in 1924 was followed by a struggle for power between Trotsky and Joseph Stalin. Stalin won. Trotzky was banished, later to be murdered by his political enemies.

Stalin, the new premier, proved to be one of the most ruthless dictators in history. Dissenters and even many of the supporters who had helped him climb to power were purged from the Communist Party. At least twenty million people were executed, and many others lived under threat of arrest. Premier Stalin was determined to carry out the avowed aim of Communism: to establish a Communist form of government in other nations, by persuasion and infiltration, if possible, but by force if necessary. When World War II ended, Soviet armies had conquered most of Eastern Europe.

By then Soviet Russia was the largest and most powerful nation in a union of more than a hundred "republics," known collectively as the Union of Soviet Socialist Republics, or the U.S.S.R. Though the satellite countries had their local soviets, important policies were decided in the Kremlin.

After Stalin's death in 1953, his successors seemed moderate in comparison. By 1967, the fiftieth anniversary of the Russian Revolution, the Soviet Union had become a superpower in the world. Officials could point with pride—and usually did, in their well-organized propaganda—to many concrete accomplishments. Though the standard of living was below that of most of Western Europe and North America, the majority of Russians were better fed and better clothed than their grandparents had been under the czars. Education and health services were free. Great advances had been made in science, but progress had been achieved at the expense of the liberties prized by citizens of the Free World. Few Russians could travel when and where they wished or change jobs without permission. Writers had to write to please Communist authorities or suffer the consequences, which usually meant prison. Any dissent was followed by more repression, and repression resulted in the flight of more refugees seeking safety elsewhere.

The first great wave of displaced persons—people who no longer had a country—had been the Russians who escaped after the 1917 revolution. Not only members of the nobility and officers in the old Imperial army, but engineers, scientists, doctors, clergymen, and men and women prominent in the arts were the special targets of abuse from the new Bolshevik masters. Those first DPs, forced to leave most of their possessions behind, wandered through the countries of Europe and Asia, and some of them found asylum in the United States.

One emigré with a sense of humor called them a generation of "formers." A former prince became a butler. A former rear admiral found a position as a janitor. Former engineers, professors, doctors, and artists became proprietors of restaurants or raised poultry and vegetables to earn a living. It was natural that they should miss Mother Russia, but the majority were able to adjust to their new circumstances.

"The life here in America," said a lady who had once lived on a big estate, "is to me like a resurrection after so many escapes from death."

An ex-patriot who helped nearly fifty thousand other ex-patriots to find a meaningful life in America was Alexandra Tolstoy, daughter of the great writer. Born a countess, she insisted on being called Miss Tolstoy after she founded the Tolstoy farm about thirty miles from New York City. Here refugee Russians could come and help work in the fields until they found jobs elsewhere.

One of the first Russian refugees to reach New York City was Igor Sikorsky, an aeronautical engineer. After he became a naturalized American citizen, he made important contributions in his field, especially in the development of helicopters. When he first arrived, though, it had been difficult to find work and he sometimes went hungry.

"But there was never a day," he said, "that I lost faith in my planes or that I did not say aloud, 'Thank God I am here, a free man, breathing free air. No man can order what I do. If I fail I can try again.' "

The most publicized of all refugees was a defector who arrived nearly a half century later. Svetlana Alliluyeva was the daughter of Joseph Stalin, but she chose to be known by the family name of her gentle mother. She had grown up believing that her father was always right, but after attending Moscow State University, where she studied American history, she gradually came to realize that he was a despot. She knew that she would always have to live with the terrifying truth that through him millions of innocent people had been destroyed.

A few years after Stalin died came the death of Brajesh Singh, a man from India with whom Svetlana was in love. Soviet authorities had refused to allow her to marry a foreigner, but she received grudging permission to carry his ashes back to India where they could be scattered over the waters of the sacred Ganges. To her, Russia had become a prison, and when the time came to return she could not bear the thought of going back. Instead, she applied at the American embassy in New Delhi for asylum in the United States. Eventually she was able to enter the country. Two books published after her arrival were amazingly successful.

"I have made many friends . . . " she wrote to an acquaintance in Paris. "I enjoy the freedom of intercourse of which I was deprived during my whole life in Russia. After being cloistered for forty years in Moscow, my life is now really free and full of interest and significance for me."

In 1970 Svetlana was married to a well-known architect, William Wesley Peters, and expected to become a citizen of the United States.

An earlier defector was Igor Gouzenko, a cipher clerk in the Soviet embassy in Ottawa, Canada. In 1945, when he and his wife Anna were due to return home, both of them were distressed by the thought that their young son, Andrei, and another child soon to be born might have to be brought up under Communism. Moreover, Gouzenko knew that spies on this side of the Atlantic were in touch with the Soviet government, which planned to betray its Allies. If he carried out his plan of defecting to the West, he would have to prove his case by taking with him certain documents to which as a cipher clerk he had access.

He was faced with a difficult decision. If he should be caught by the NKVD, the Soviet secret police, what would happen to his family? The following excerpt is condensed from the book of the same title.

This Was My Choice (1945)

BY IGOR GOUZENKO

It was an unseasonably hot and sultry night as I walked back to the military attache's. But I knew the perspiration trickling inside my shirt was caused by more than the weather. Tonight was to be the turning point of my life, and the lives of my family, from Soviet slavery to democratic freedom. The deadline had been forced by my superior's abrupt decision for me to turn over my work to my successor, Lieutenant Koulakov, in the very near future.

I am no hero. I was born a very ordinary little man of Russia. But that night of September 5, 1945, I came as close to becoming a hero as I ever will.

This could be, I was fully aware, my last night on earth. One wrong move could mean the complete ruination of all our plans and, as far as I was aware, the NKVD might have been watching me for some time. There was an easier, a vastly safer way out than by going back for those documents. Yet somehow, I managed to freeze my mind into the course Anna and I had mapped out.

We had decided long since that it would be necessary to make my escape during a weekday, although a Saturday night would have been ideal, allowing me until Monday morning to make good my getaway. But the newspaper offices would not be open Saturday night, and we had decided I should take the documents and my story to a newspaper.

There was no thought of going to the police. That was a natural result of our experience with the thoroughly corrupt

NKVD police. I naturally thought the local police would sell out to the Soviet Embassy. At the same time, we had been impressed with the freedom and fearlessness of the Canadian press.

Reaching the Soviet embassy that Wednesday night, I nodded to the guard, who nodded in return as I signed the book. As I was putting my fountain pen back in my pocket I glanced toward the reception room and my blood seemed to freeze.

There sat Vitali Pavlov, chief of the NKVD in Canada!

Somehow I managed to act naturally and walked by the reception room seemingly concerned with the clip of my pen not fastening into my pocket the way it should. From the corner of my eye I noted that Pavlov apparently had failed to notice me. I mounted the stairs leading to the secret cipher room, pressed the secret bell under the banister, pulled aside the curtain, and held my face in front of the small opening in the steel door.

The attendant inside unbarred the steel door. It was Ryazanov, commercial attaché cipher clerk and a friend of mine. I noted with relief that he was alone.

We exchanged a few remarks on the weather. Ryazanov asked if I was working late again.

"No," I replied, "there are just a couple of telegrams to do and then I'll catch an eight-thirty movie."

Ryazanov said I was being sensible and turned to his own work.

I entered my little office and closed the door carefully behind me. I went to my desk, opened it, and removed the cipher pouch, which I had left there that afternoon. Most of the documents I wanted were there. The others were in the files. All were marked by the turned-down corners.

Some of the documents were large sheets of paper. Others were small scraps. Later, the police count showed a hundred and nine items.

I opened my shirt and carefully distributed the documents

inside. Then I completed the telegrams which represented my reason for being there. I walked across the corridor and handed them to Ryazanov for dispatching to Moscow. Though to me my shirt appeared to bulge suspiciously, he displayed no undue interest. Casually I stepped into the men's room and washed my hands.

"It's too hot to stick around here," I called out. "Why don't you skip out with me to the show?"

Ryazanov grunted. "Fat chance of getting away with anything around here. Besides, Pavlov is downstairs. Thanks just the same; I'd better stick around."

Mention of Pavlov left me a little weak around the knees. I had momentarily forgotten him. But there was no turning back now. I adjusted my shirt again and stepped to the door. Ryazanov opened it and I bade him good night.

I was careful about walking down the steps, afraid that I might disturb the documents and cause an extra large bulge. There was also danger that a smaller document might slip through my belt and drop from a pant leg on the floor.

Sweat was standing out on my brow, and I felt my chest tightening as I approached the reception room. I didn't even dare reach into a pocket for my handkerchief lest the movement disturb something.

The street door seemed miles away. Gradually I neared the reception room. Then I was passing it. My heart leaped with joy. The room was empty. Pavlov had gone. A good omen. I was very much in luck. I signed myself out in the book, bade the attendant good night, and walked out into the night. It was still humid but I sucked in the air gratefully.

I took a streetcar downtown and went quickly to the office of the *Ottawa Journal* newspaper. Outside the building I stopped to mop my brow and make sure nobody was following me. Finally, I entered and asked the elevator man where I could find the editor.

"Sixth floor," he said, and slammed the door shut behind me.

At the sixth floor I walked toward the door marked "Editor," but just as I was about to knock grim doubts filled my mind. Surely, I thought, every big newspaper must have an NKVD agent working in it. Was I doing the right thing? Hurriedly I decided to think it over and turned back to the elevator. The door opened to let somebody out and the operator yelled, "Down!"

I stepped in. The elevator descended a few floors and stopped to pick up some people. Among them was a girl who looked at me and smiled.

"What are you doing here? Is there news breaking at the embassy?"

I was panic-stricken. Her face was familiar. Where had I seen her before?

The elevator reached the ground floor. As the door opened I muttered an apology to the girl, said something about being in a big hurry, and walked quickly to the street. Outside I ran to the first corner and then slowed to a fast walk. What would I do now? I boarded a streetcar and went home. When Anna answered my code knock, her face was white and drawn.

"Did something go wrong?" she whispered.

I sat down heavily on the sofa and told her of being spotted by the girl in the elevator.

"Don't worry about her, Igor." Anna's voice came absolutely unruffled. "She must be a journalist or she would not have been in the office. Many journalists have been entertained at the embassy and that is where she probably met you. But even if there is an NKVD agent in the newspaper office, what could he do in time to stop you? Go back and see the editor. You still have several hours before the embassy learns what has happened."

Taking renewed strength from her confidence, I opened my shirt and removed the documents. They were soaked with sweat. Anna tried to dry them a bit by waving them. Then she wrapped them in a paper.

Anna kissed me as she opened the door. I squeezed her arm and went out into the night again. At the *Ottawa Journal* the same elevator man took me up to the sixth floor. I stepped quickly to the editor's door and knocked. There was no answer. I walked down to a door leading into a large room. It was the City Room, filled with busy people. Then I saw an office boy hurrying in my direction. I asked him where I could find the editor.

"Gone for the night," he said as he dashed past.

I walked to the nearest desk and told a man working at a typewriter that I wished to see whoever was in charge. "It is extremely important."

He looked at me inquiringly, but said nothing. Then he took me over to a desk at the other side of the big room where an older man wearing a green eyeshade told me to sit down. I took out the stolen documents and spread them on the desk. As I did so, I explained who I was and that these were proof that Soviet agents in Canada were seeking data on the atomic bomb.

The man with the eyeshade stared at me, then picked up several of the documents. But he looked at them only for a moment. They were written in Russian.

"I'm sorry," he said finally. "This is out of our field. I would suggest you go to the Royal Canadian Mounted Police or come back in the morning to see the editor."

I hastened to explain that by morning the NKVD might be on my trail and even kill me. But as I spoke my heart was falling. I could see from the man's expression that he thought I was crazy.

"Sorry," he said. "I'm busy."

He stood up and walked away, leaving me sitting there. I felt helpless and confused. Out on the street I leaned against the wall and tried to collect my thoughts. There was only one thing to do and that was contact a high official. The Minister of Justice seemed the logical person. I walked to the Justice Building on Wellington Street, where a tall man in R.C.M.P. uniform stopped me at the door. I hesitated for a moment but realized things were getting desperate. I said it was most important that I see the Minister of Justice immediately.

The policeman replied politely but firmly. "I'm sorry. It is almost midnight. You can see nobody until morning."

Sorry! That word was getting on my nerves. "But," I repeated, "it is desperately necessary that I reach the Minister right away—by telephone at least."

He shook his head. "It can't be done."

I returned home, more than a little frightened. Anna, however, bolstered me again.

"Don't worry about it. You have the whole morning to reach the Minister. Have a good sleep and you will feel better."

She tucked the documents in her handbag and put it under her pillow. But neither of us slept that night. We just lay there thinking and talking until the first light of dawn was filtering through our bedroom window.

"Anna," I said, "we will all go to the Minister of Justice's office as soon as it opens, around nine o'clock. I might be kept waiting and the suspense would be unbearable if I wasn't certain about your safety. I'll dress Andrei. Do you think you could stand the strain?"

"I will be all right," she replied instantly. "We will all go together."

We decided that she should carry the documents in her purse, because if the NKVD caught up with us they would go after me. I would try to create a diversion and Anna, with our little son, might have a chance to slip away. The documents would be a passport to protective custody with the Canadian government, I thought.

At the Justice Building, I explained to the man at the reception desk that I had to see the Minister of Justice on a matter of great urgency. The man looked at me doubtfully, then spoke for some time into the telephone. We were escorted to the

Minister's office, where a courteous secretary asked the nature of my business.

I did my best to tell him the matter was of such importance that I dared not speak to anybody but the Minister. The secretary glanced from me to Anna to little Andrei. I could imagine what was running through his mind: this man may be off his head but if that is the case why would he bring along his wife and child? I had not thought of that angle in my planning, but it seemed a fortunate one. The secretary went into the inside office, and I could hear him telephoning somebody.

The secretary finally returned.

"The Minister is in his other office over in the Parliament Buildings," he said. "I will take you there."

We went over to Parliament Hill and through the picturesque halls to the Minister's office. But I had to see another secretary first. It was the same thing all over again. I had to speak to the Minister personally; nobody else would do. The secretary picked up his telephone and talked to somebody at length—in French. I knew it was about me because I heard my name mentioned, but I could not understand anything else. After some time he hung up the telephone and told the first secretary to take us back to the Justice Building and wait there for the Minister.

Back we went and sat there for two precious hours. Andrei was getting impatient and we had trouble keeping him from crying. The telephone rang. The secretary listened and said, "Very well, sir," then turned to us.

"I am very sorry. The Minister is unable to see you."

Sorry? Again that word! I looked at Anna with a hint of panic.

She was biting her lip. "Let us go to the newspaper office again," she said.

The editor wasn't available, we were told on arrival at the *Ottawa Journal*. But a girl reporter was sent out to talk to us. She listened intently, looking at Anna repeatedly as if seeking confirmation. She studied the documents momentarily, then took them into the editor's office. Within a very short time she came out.

"I am terribly sorry," she said, handing me back the documents. "Your story just doesn't seem to register here."

It was Anna who spoke first. "What should we do now, Miss?"

The girl reporter pondered. "Why not go to see the R.C.M.P. about taking out naturalization papers? That should prevent the Reds from taking you back."

In utter desperation we returned to the Justice Building. An officer at the police identification branch said the R.C.M.P. had nothing to do with naturalization and told us to go to the Crown Attorney's office.

We had quite a distance to go and the day was getting hot. It suddenly dawned on me that we hadn't eaten since early morning. I took Anna and Andrei to a little restaurant near the courthouse building where the Crown Attorney's office was located. By now, it was fifteen minutes to two and I could imagine what was happening at the embassy. But perhaps they hadn't yet noticed the missing documents and were merely wondering why I hadn't shown up for work.

Andrei fell asleep at the table. Anna then decided we had better take the child to a friend of hers, a British woman in the next building to ours. It was risky, but we just couldn't get around with the tired child. We got on a streetcar and went back to our street. The neighbor was most kind when Anna stated she had to do some shopping before returning to Moscow. The child would be all right until we returned, she said.

Back we went to the Crown Attorney's office. The girl gave us forms to fill out, then told us to return next day to arrange for photographs. I looked at her in alarm.

"How long will this naturalization take?"

"Oh," she replied, "I can't tell you for sure. A few months, perhaps."

Anna burst into tears. It was the first time her courage had failed her. I put an arm around her and spoke in Russian. Miserably, I looked around the office. There, at another desk, was a woman in a red dress. Just what I saw in her expression I don't know but, on sudden impulse, I moved quickly across the room and poured out my story to her.

She listened in obvious amazement, then stood up and brought over a couple of chairs. I noted the name plate on her desk: Mrs. Fernande Joubarne.

"This is something the world should know," she said firmly. "I will try to help you."

Anna grasped my hand as Mrs. Joubarne telephoned another newspaper. I heard her telling somebody there was a "story" in her office of "world importance" and suggested a reporter be sent immediately. In about half an hour a male reporter appeared, and again I related my story. I translated the documents for him, and he asked me to repeat the parts about the atomic bomb. Finally he shook his head.

"It's too big for us to handle—much too big. It is a matter for the police or the government. I suggest you take it to them."

Mrs. Joubarne sighed. "There is nothing more I can do. You had better follow his advice." Then, to Anna she said, "And good luck to you. Let me know if it is a boy or a girl."

We walked out into the blazing afternoon sun. I stopped at the foot of the stairs, not knowing which way to turn.

Anna took my arm. "Let us go home, Igor," she said, an immense weariness in her voice.

The danger of going home didn't mean anthing to me any more. I was near total exhaustion, and home at least meant rest, somewhere to plan what to do next. As we neared our street I told Anna to go into the next building for Andrei while I went up to our apartment. If all was well I would wave to her across the areaway between the buildings.

I went up the stairs and listened at our apartment door. Everything was quiet. I unlocked the door and looked inside. Everything seemed in order. I stepped out onto the rear balcony. All was clear. Anna was already looking from the friend's window, and I waved for her to come home.

After she returned with Andrei I lay down across the bed, but sleep wouldn't come. After a short time I got up and walked to one of the front windows. As I looked down, my heart skipped a beat!

Two men were seated on a bench in the park directly opposite, and both were looking up at my window!

I stepped back farther from the curtain so my shadow wouldn't be seen. Every little while they would look up at the apartment and then resume conversation. At that moment there was a knock on the apartment door, and I signaled for Anna to remain quiet. There was another knock, louder and more insistent. This was repeated four times. The person outside had apparently decided to call it a day, but Andrei chose that moment to dash across the living room.

A fist banged harshly on the door. A voice rasped, "Gouzenko!"

I recognized the voice. It belonged to one of the men at the embassy, and he called my name several times. Then we heard his footsteps going down the stairs. When I returned to the front window, the men sitting on the park bench were still there, occasionally looking up.

The clock said 7:05. That meant Sergeant Harold Main of the Royal Canadian Air Force who lived next door would be at home. I hurried out to the rear balcony. Main and his wife were seated there seeking relief from the heat. I asked Sergeant Main if I could speak to him. "Sure," he said, and I asked him if he and his wife would take care of little Andrei if something happened suddenly to Anna and me.

The sergeant showed surprise. Then he beckoned me to come over the railing and follow him inside. I felt there wasn't much time to talk so I boiled everything down to the fact that Anna and I expected an attempt to be made on our lives by the NKVD and we were worried about the boy. Sergeant Main looked at me doubtfully, but his expression changed when I pointed out the men on the park bench. As he led the way back out onto the rear balcony, he stopped short. There was a man in the areaway looking up!

Sergeant Main made up his mind promptly.

"Get your wife and boy, Gouzenko, and bring them over here. I'm going to get the police."

The idea of consulting the police no longer alarmed me. The capable, assured manner of my Air Force friend carried a confident impression that everything would soon be all right.

I climbed back onto our balcony and entered the house. The door was open—Anna and Andrei were gone!

Rushing through the doorway and into the hall, I stopped short, somewhat abashed on seeing them in the apartment directly across the way talking to a Mrs. Francis Elliott, who lived there.

After listening to our story, Mrs. Elliott suggested we stay with her for the night because her husband and son were away and there was a daybed we could use. She would find a place for Andrei.

I accepted her kindness gratefully. While Anna and Mrs. Elliott were talking I sat down in the dining room, feeling rather spent. Before long, heavy footsteps sounded in the hall. It was Sergeant Main, with two Ottawa constables, who assured me they would keep the building under observation all night. Mrs. Elliott made up the daybed and suggested we get some much-needed rest.

Sometime between eleven-thirty and midnight Anna and I woke with a start. There was a sound of knocking on our apartment door across the hallway. I slipped out of bed and over to the door. Through the keyhole, I could see our door clearly. Knocking on it was Pavlov, the NKVD chief, and with him were three other men from the embassy. As I watched I heard Sergeant Main's door open. I could hear him asking what they wanted. One of the four mentioned my name. The sergeant replied, "The Gouzenkos are away."

Pavlov thanked him and the four went downstairs.

Anna squeezed my arm as I made a motion to move away. "Keep still," she whispered, "they're coming back!"

I looked through the keyhole once more and saw Pavlov working on our door with a jimmy. There was a rasping sound when the door opened. The four entered and shut the door quietly behind them.

Mrs. Elliott tiptoed beside me. Then she phoned the police and reported that somebody was trying to break into the apartment across the hall from hers.

In an unbelievably short space of time, the same two constables appeared at my apartment door. One of them, Constable Thomas Walsh, didn't wait for any formality but threw open the door. He and the other policeman, Constable John McCulloch, caught the four men in the act of rifling my desk and bureau drawers.

We opened Mrs. Elliott's door a crack and listened. Constable Walsh had apparently asked for an explanation, and Pavlov said in crisp, official tones, "This apartment belongs to a fellow member of the Soviet embassy, a man named Gouzenko, who happens to be in Toronto tonight. He left some documents here and we have his permission to look for them."

Constable Walsh's tone was just as official.

"Did he also give you permission to break his lock?" He pointed to the twisted lock. "Was this done with your bare hands?"

Pavlov waxed indignant.

"How dare you talk to me like that? We had a key for this apartment but lost it. Anyway, this lock is Soviet property and we can do what we like with it. I order you to leave."

Walsh looked at McCulloch, then back to Pavlov. "Constable McCulloch," said Walsh, "insists we remain here until the Inspector arrives. I hope you don't mind. Meanwhile, let me see your identification!"

An Inspector Macdonald finally came and queried the four more extensively. Pavlov was fuming. He charged the constables had insulted them and that Soviet diplomatic immunity had been assailed. When he ordered his three companions to leave with him, no effort was made to stop them.

In the morning another Ottawa city police inspector visited us. He said the Royal Canadian Mounted Police would like to have a talk with me at the Justice Building.

Anna gave a big, deep sigh of relief. "At last, Igor, at last," she said. "They are going to listen to you."

As I hurried into my coat, I looked at Anna. She appeared pale and nervous. "What are you going to do while I am at the Justice Building?" I asked. Anna's reply was typical.

"I have a big washing to do. Don't worry about me, Igor."

My reception at the Justice Building was a marked constrast to my visits of the previous day. High-ranking Royal Canadian Mounted Police and civilian investigators were waiting. They treated me most courteously and, for almost five hours, I answered their questions. The documents aroused considerable interest and discussion after they had listened to my translation.

When I described my difficulty in trying to get somebody to listen to me, one of the R.C.M.P. officers smiled. "You weren't quite as neglected as you thought," he said to me.

"That's a fine way to talk," one of the civilian investigators added, "after my partner and I spent so much time sitting in the park watching your apartment."

So the two men had been Canadian policemen and not NKVD men, as I had suspected. Actually, during the two hours Anna, Andrei, and I had waited outside the Justice Minister's office, the Canadian Department of External Affairs and the R.C.M.P. had been pondering over what to do with me. Prime Minister Mackenzie King was consulted. It had been decided to "shadow" me for a few days to judge by developments whether I was what I claimed to be or just a mental case suffering from an anti-Red complex. It was realized, too, that if I was bona fide the case would be an international hot coal to handle.

From then on we were heavily guarded by the R.C.M.P., but anxious hours lay ahead of us. Anna's pregnancy called for intensive planning, since I knew Pavlov was aware of her condition and would be watching the hospitals for miles around. So, one night in December, it was arranged that a Royal Canadian Mounted Police constable should take her to a hospital, where he posed as the father. By pretending to be an illiterate foreigner he managed to overcome much of the red tape demanded in making out official forms. He said, in broken English, that he was a Polish farmer and Anna also pretended to be Polish, with very little knowledge of the English language.

The baby was a girl. Two days after she was born, a passing nurse stopped by Anna's bed and exclaimed, "Why, hello there, you! Don't you remember me? I took care of you in Ottawa when you had another baby."

Anna was petrified with fear but somehow managed to play her role. She was a Polish farmer's wife. She had never been to Ottawa. Then her "husband" appeared, and apparently the nurse thought she had made a mistake. There was no sequel to the incident, but we were worried.

In the years that have passed since then I have emerged for the various espionage trials—some twenty of them, I believe —but only under heavy guard. The R.C.M.P. are taking no chances with Pavlov's long memory and the equally long memory of the NKVD. There might be a time when they can relax, and Anna and I can enter normal existence with our children.

Life in hiding can never be ideal, but there has been sunshine, too. I had no thought, in making my break, of any financial returns to be derived from it. But a prominent Ottawa businessman provided me with an annuity for life. An American magazine paid handsomely for a partial story of my disclosures on Soviet espionage, and Hollywood has seen fit to make a movie involving Anna and me. In my leisure hours I have

been painting, and some of those paintings have already gone
on exhibition in a number of cities.

Yes, fate has been kind beyond all expectations. If I had it all
to do over again, with no hope of financial benefits or even
security for my family, I would make the break again. I am now
only a small but happy pebble on the democratic beach, but
no one appreciates more the wonders of democratic citizenship than I do. When the Canadian government by special
Order-in-Council conferred citizenship upon me, I thought it
was the most wonderful gift in the world.

The greatest gain is the one I feel deep down inside: that I
did my duty toward the millions enslaved and voiceless in
Russia today. Letters have come to me from all parts of the
United States, Canada, Europe, and even India which warm
my heart. There is one, in particular, which comes from a
displaced persons' camp. It is dated November 12, 1947, Hano-
ver, Germany, and the writer says he is a former Soviet citizen
from the Ukraine.

"Dear Igor Gouzenko," the letter reads in part. "At the
beginning of 1946 we heard with great joy about your important decision made in the interests of the world in general and
people like us in particular. . . . By uncovering Stalin's espionage ring you seriously hindered his key tool toward his goal
of world domination. . . . We political refugees have tried to
warn people of Stalin's aims. Now at last the democracies of the
world are beginning to wake up. . . ."

It was heartwarming, too, to hear from Mackenzie King,
Prime Minister of Canada: "The people of Canada and the
world are your debtors."

All this makes me convinced I shall live to see the day when
the Russian people will delight in the same freedom I first saw
in Canada, the freedom which inspired and gave me the
strength to take the big step. The opportunity I was given to
serve my people will not be granted all sons of Russia, but I
think it is promising that such a small cog as myself in the vast
Soviet machine could have done so much.

Ironically enough, it was Pavlov's jimmying open of my apartment door that convinced the authorities Igor Gouzenko really had a story to tell.

*   *   *

Mrs. Gouzenko also had an interesting story to tell about the family's life in Canada since the dramatic events of 1945. "Igor and I have too much of a foreign accent to pose as native-born Canadians," she said, "but our friends and our two children have no idea that we were born in the Soviet Union. They think we came to Canada from another country in Europe. But we are not lonely. Under our assumed name we have made many friends, and the freedom in America never ceases to amaze people like us who grew up in a Communist police state. Democracy has indeed been good to us. I think we are the luckiest couple in the world."

12

Czech Refugees

For several centuries after the religious wars of the 1600s the Czechs, or Bohemians, and their Slovak neighbors were a part of the Austro-Hungarian Empire, but in spirit they remained fiercely independent. During World War I a "Free Czechoslovakia" movement was promoted by a Czech patriot and scholar, Thomas Masaryk, who spent some time in the United States winning the support of Americans of Czech descent. He also won the approval of President Woodrow Wilson, and when the old Austro-Hungarian Empire was broken up, as a result of the Allied victory in 1918, a dream of centuries was realized. The independent republic of Czechoslovakia was proclaimed, and Masaryk became its first president.

The government of the young republic was one of the most democratic in Europe until Adolf Hitler, the Nazi Führer, threatened the peace of the world. In 1938 he demanded that part of the new nation's territory be annexed to Germany. The leaders of France and England, both allies of Czechoslovakia, agreed, hoping in this way to prevent another war, but their concessions proved futile. World War II began the following year.

"Was it conceivable," said one Czech who had found a refuge in America, "that little more than a year has passed since we belonged to free, democratic Czechoslovakia? We had watched Hitler's increasing campaign against 'our' country, and when his threats assumed a roaring and thunderous volume we knew what that meant. We packed and stood ready. We waited. One evening the shout went up: " 'The Nazis are coming!'

"Now we realized how people must have felt fifteen hundred years

136

ago when the terrified cries of 'The Huns! The Huns!' had swept over Europe."

During the World War II all of Czechoslovakia was occupied by Nazi troops until they were driven out by the victorious Allies in 1945. Three years later, Communists seized control of the government, and one tyranny was replaced by another. Every movement of the people was watched, and children were expected to inform on parents who disagreed with the Communist Party line.

"We thought of little else except how we could escape," said one man, "and take our families with us."

Escape was increasingly difficult as police regulations were tightened. But some escapees did succeed, often at great sacrifices of the underground workers who helped them. The Czechs became more restless as time passed, and more resentful of the government policies dictated by Soviet Russia. In 1968, Alexander Dubcek, the premier, in an attempt to introduce such reforms as freedom of speech, of the press, and of assembly, was supported by the majority of his people. Their efforts to gain some measure of liberty, however, were ruthlessly put down in 1968 by an invasion of Soviet troops, aided by the forces of several Russian satellite countries. Dubcek was ousted from office, and a new wave of refugees attempted to flee the country.

The selection that follows is by a courageous nun who had escaped some years earlier.

The Deliverance of Sister Cecelia (1952)

AS TOLD TO WILLIAM BRINKLEY

I feel someone shaking me hard enough to hurt, and I wake up in my room in the children's hospital in Bratislava and see it is a sister, all pale and quivering. "Four policemen are waiting for you downstairs," she wails, "and there are four automobiles full of them outside. Mother Superior says to take a blanket with you, because it will be cold at the police station."

"Sister," I say, "I don't plan to go to the police station."

I go to my trunk and get out a dress, a dark blue dress with white polka dots, and a blue kerchief. A woman whose child was at the hospital gave it to me in case such a day as this should come. I put on the dress and tie the kerchief around my head. I grab some old rags to carry, so I will look like a hospital maid. I go downstairs, out through a side door, and walk straight through a line of police. They do not even look at me twice.

So, after months of helping other people hide and escape across the border, I myself am the one in hiding. Now I would live like an animal, fleeing from hole to hole. It would be four months before I crossed the border at last, on a night of darkness and fear—the ninth of January, 1952.

For an agent of the Underground the Holy Savior picked a strange one in me. I was born in a town in Slovakia so small you could count the houses, and when I was seventeen I decided to go into a convent. My entrance into the work of the Underground began when the Communists imprisoned Father Matthew, a priest who came from my home town. I sent him some food packages, and when he escaped I helped him hide. Afterward I helped him find someone who, for a price—a good one, too—took him and two other priests across the border.

So I became an underground worker in a Communist country, and I knew that soon the police must come for me. But if God kisses you, you receive the golden gift of a moment's warning. I had God and the blue polka-dot dress when the police came in September—two days after I had aided the escape of a priest who had been condemned to be hanged.

Dusk is just beginning as I walk through the police lines from the hospital, carrying with me into this new life nothing from the old but two pictures—a stained picture of St. Joseph and a picture of the Virgin Mary that I have had from the time I became a nun. The guilt and the fear I feel! Guilt because in the twenty-one years since I took my holy vows I was not wearing my nun's habit. And fear of being captured. For they do their worst of all to those who have helped people escape. I have never known anything near physical torture and do not know how much I can bear, even if God is with me. So, as though into the midst of the shadow of death, I walk down the street.

Where to go? I decide that I will first try Vera's apartment. She is an old friend of mine, and she lives with three other girls. When I come in they do not recognize me. Then they realize who it is and cry out, "Sister! The dress!"

"The police are after me; give me one night."

All the girls except Vera leave the apartment quickly. I understand, for they know what the Communists do if you are caught hiding a person. Vera stays with me, but next morning she goes to her work. I stay in the apartment until dark. Then I start out again, leaving a note telling her where I am going. My plan is to stay for a while with the family of some children I taught at the convent. I walk through side streets to get to their house.

The husband, Dominic, answers the bell. He is a tall, skinny man. When he recognizes me he says quickly that his wife and children are away visiting her parents. What do I want? I explain. He starts shivering.

"May I stay overnight?" I ask. "Just one night?"

"Y-e-s," he croaks.

He goes over to the windows and pulls down the blinds. He keeps peeking out to the street from behind them. All night he sits in a chair in the living room. So I sit up, too, and through the blinds I see the dawn come. I remember this will be the first Sunday that I have ever missed Mass, and I feel a great loneliness.

But I feel better later in the morning when Vera comes. She

is a brave girl, and she promises to go to see a nun whose parents live out in the country and ask if I can stay with them for a while. She is away three hours and I begin to worry when finally the door bell rings. Dominic starts shaking all over and jumps behind the couch. I peek out the window and see Vera standing on the steps—and with her is Sister Margaret! I open the door and Margaret and I fall into each other's arms.

"You should not have come, Sister Margaret!" I say, bringing them inside. "It is very dangerous. I only want you to let me go to your parents."

"Nonsense," she says. "I'll take you."

She tells me how the police searched the hospital the whole night after I left. She has brought me my rosary, my cross, and my prayer book. When I take them from her it is like a new strength passing into my hands.

Vera also has brought some other, quite different, things: a new green silk dress of hers that is much better than the worn blue polka dot, a green kerchief, some shoes with high heels, and some silk stockings.

I put on the green dress and the silk stockings. I try on the high-heeled shoes, but when I start across the room I almost fall. So I put on the plain flat shoes I have worn since becoming a nun.

Vera reaches into her purse. "Now the rouge and lipstick," she says. "And polish for the fingernails."

"No, no!" I say. "What will St. Joseph think?"

"Give St. Joseph credit for a little sense," says Sister Margaret. "With rouge and lipstick and fingernail polish no one will ever guess that you are a nun."

But I cannot consent to this, even if the Communists should get me. I cannot, and finally Sister Margaret gives up her arguments.

Then she gives me the plan. She will be at the railroad station at eight. I am not to speak to her but follow at a distance. I stay at Dominic's house all that day until dark. When I leave he is very happy to see me go.

In the station I find Sister Margaret. I follow her to her house. Sister Margaret's parents wish to keep me, but it is not safe there, for they have a Communist neighbor. So they call Anna, Margaret's sister.

Anna is a very pretty girl with eyes that flame when she gets angry, as she does now when she is told about me. She is almost more upset than I am because I have to hide. She goes to find me a new hiding place.

This one is in the same house where Father Matthew hid out. It is miles away, but Anna walks there and back the same day and brings this answer: hurry on. I tell Sister Margaret goodbye —how it hurts to leave her!—and after dark I start out. Alone, I walk to my new hiding place.

The house belongs to two elderly sisters, Helena and Rose, who make their living doing embroidery. They devote themselves to hiding people. They know that the police will one day get them. One of them, Rose, smiles when I ask her about that.

"So they take the last few years of my life," she says. "So? By this I buy dozens of years of life for other people."

These two tiny old ladies have a helper, a dog named Gastan. He is the size of a Shetland pony and has the manners of a hungry tiger. He runs free in the fenced yard. The bell to the house is on the outside of the gate. If a visitor rings the bell, Gastan sets up a roar like something out of the jungle of Africa. One of the old sisters goes to the door and speaks gently to the visitor. "Just a minute, if you please, while I put Gastan away." Then she opens the door and this huge monster bounds into the house, and the sisters lock him in the kitchen. Only then do they let the visitor in.

All of this takes at least five minutes and assures me plenty of time to get into the hideout. The hideout is a tiny room with a bathtub in it which just about fills the entire room and is the only place to sit. The door has no knob on the outside and fits flush into the wall. When I am inside and the door is closed the two sisters together pull and push an enormous clothes cupboard across the door, covering it completely.

In the manner of old ladies they have a number of harmless visitors their own age who have nothing more to do than pass the time with them. So I spend many an hour in the bathtub, so many that I start keeping some sewing and the Holy Gospel in the bathtub to give me something to do and read.

One day several weeks after my arrival Gastan starts barking and Rose peeks out the window.

"Hide, Sister, hide!" she says, and by the way she says it I know it is not just another lady friend calling. I run fast into the little room and sit in the bathtub and the sisters shut the door behind me and then pull the cupboard across it. After a while I can hear Gastan leaping into the house and the kitchen door close behind him. Then I hear the feet of many men tramping all over the house. After a while I hear them open the door of the cupboard which stands against the door to my hideout. I can clearly hear them rustling through the clothes. In the bathtub I hold my breath and pray to St. Joseph. I hear voices raised.

Then all is silent.

It is a while before I hear the cupboard being pulled away. It sounds as if the two old ladies are having a great trouble pulling it away. Then it is away enough for me to get out and I see why: only Rose is there to pull and push it.

"Where is Helena?" I ask, feeling hollow inside me, for I think I already know.

"They took Helena," Rose says quietly. "Sister," she asks, "why didn't they take me instead?"

Then she is all business again very quickly. "Sister, it will be dangerous for you here now. I must take you somewhere else."

So that night she walks through the country with me, and I try to think of something to say to her. But Rose touches my cheek, so gently, and she tells me, "Do not cry, Sister. To be taken in God's work—what could be better than that?"

It is not considered safe for Sister Cecilia to draw attention to herself by staying in one place for long at a time, so during the next few months she seeks shelter in several different homes. She is much frightened when a man in a policeman's uniform appears, but he assures her that he is really Father Joseph, who recently escaped from a Communist prison. He now goes about in disguise helping his countrymen who are in danger escape from Czechoslovakia. A few days later another underground worker, Father Philip, wearing the uniform of a Communist official, also calls on her and tells her she must board the afternoon train the next day. Both Father Joseph and Father Philip will be on the same train, this time disguised as workingmen. She must show no sign of recognition but follow them when they leave at a certain station.

From the station Father Philip leads us out into a small woods and tells us to wait. He has to meet two more trains. After a while Father Philip returns with four young men, who are students for the priesthood, and a tall man carrying binoculars. The tall man will be our first leader.

Before we go, we kneel in the dark woods on the frozen ground and receive from Father Philip a blessing. "God bless you and be with you on all your crossings and all your roads."

After Father Philip leaves us, we follow our leader through the dark, until after some hours we come to a house on the edge of a small town. Here a woman holding a watchdog by the collar lets us in the back door. The leader leaves us in the kitchen, where we pass the rest of the night huddled around a wood stove. There is one bed in the kitchen but no one sleeps. To keep warmer I go into a little storage room next to the kitchen and change into my ski pants.

All the next day we stay in that house. At midnight the door opens and there is the tall man with the binoculars and eleven other people. Six of these are priesthood students. The other five are a family of a mother, a father, two children, and the mother's brother. The girl, Katherine, is four years old and the boy, Mike, is seven. It pains my heart to look at them and to think that such little children are going on this kind of journey.

That night the mother, the two children, and I are given the bed in the kitchen. I tell the children stories until they get sleepy. Then I lie down by the three of them.

The man who comes for us the next morning is Joseph, and we soon call him Big Jo Jo. He is to be our leader in the attempt to cross the border. The man with the binoculars we now call Little Jo Jo, even though he's actually taller, because he is the No. 2 leader.

All day we stay in the house. The day is passed in checking the things that are to help us cross the border. Little Jo Jo takes out a rubber boat from a big bag and blows it up with a pump, and Big Jo Jo goes all over it with his hands. He has very big, hairy, rough hands, but they are soft and careful as a woman's as he inspects the boat. Big Jo Jo uncoils two large rolls of clothesline, each about two hundred yards long and as thick as a small finger. Then he takes his pistol apart and cleans it. The eyes of the priesthood students grow big as they watch him.

That night we have a last meal of goulash. We get ready to leave at seven, a little after dark.

The woman of the house looks out the windows and she comes back to us in the kitchen. "Two policemen are standing on the street."

Big Jo Jo sighs. "I guess everyone can rest a little longer."

Every few minutes Big Jo Jo keeps going to look out the front window. After an hour of this, I see he is getting impatient.

"We can't wait any longer," he says. "Let's get ready."

Just then the woman comes into the kitchen and says, "They have gone."

Now Big Jo Jo stands up before us in the kitchen. His cap is cocked back a little on his head.

"Before we go," he says, "I want everyone to understand that I'm the leader. You do as I say. This trip is not a picnic at any point. But there is one point of danger above all others—the dike."

Then he tells about the dike.

The border is actually at the river Morava, which is perhaps a mile beyond the dike. But the dike, being elevated and about ninety miles long, makes a good barrier and is patrolled by men and dogs. Two teams of a man and a dog apiece have a certain section of the dike to patrol. The teams meet in the center of their section; each team walks to the end of the section, then walks back until they meet, and then repeat. Our problem will be to wait until the guards are at either end of their beat and then try to scramble across.

"There is only one other thing to understand," Big Jo Jo says. "Last week a whole party was caught and two killed. It is an excellent chance that all of us will be dead or, what is perhaps worse, caught. Anyone afraid of getting killed or caught had better stay here. Now is the time to speak up."

He pauses. No one speaks.

Suddenly Big Jo Jo takes his cap off for the first time. I am startled to hear this gruff man say, "Let us pray before we go."

We all join in the Lord's Prayer. At the end Jo Jo prays, "Our Father in heaven save us on this journey which we are going to start right now amen let's go," and he pops on his cap and opens the back door. We step out into the night and start through the brush.

We have just barely started when we hear a dog bark behind us. We look back and see the house we have just left lighted up. We do not stop to find out why.

(Later, when we were across the border, I got a letter which told me that a big party of policemen had raided the house. The two policemen who had been stationed out in front apparently had gone to get reinforcements for the raid. St. Joseph was surely with us again.)

The night lies bright on the land. The ground is speckled with snow. It has begun to thaw a little, and as we start through a marsh I can feel the water leaking into my shoes. The students carry the rubber boat, which is heavy, and the two big coils of clothesline. The men take turns carrying little four-year-old Katherine, and much of the time she is asleep in their arms. Two men lead her brother Mike by the hands. Now and then the children whimper a little. Big Jo Jo is concerned; one loud wail and all nineteen of us might be in the hands of the dike patrol.

Soon a full moon comes up, shining on the fields and glistening off the little ridges of snow that cling to the soil. It makes everything we are leaving behind beautiful. It is approaching midnight when suddenly we see in the far-off distance, rising up out of the moonlit fields, the black form of the dike.

Big Jo Jo makes us wait, lying low on the ground, while he takes the binoculars from Little Jo Jo and goes ahead to scout. We lie still and look at the dike. I think that beyond it lies freedom, but on it walks death.

Then Big Jo Jo is back. We move forward again, though much more slowly than before. The moon shines so brightly that we can even make out the color of each other's eyes.

"It's too bright," I suddenly hear Big Jo Jo mutter.

I remember St. Joseph himself was once in a situation very similar to ours. So I speak to him under my breath. "Big Jo Jo says the moon is too bright. Can't you make it a little darker? Do you remember when you were told to take little Jesus and His Mother by night into Egypt to escape Herod? Do you remember that you fled across the border exactly like us? Please help us the same way you got help when you fled. All we are asking is what you got yourself." And I pat the picture of St. Joseph through my coat.

We are going forward very slowly all the time but still are some distance from the dike. Then a strange thing happens. Looking at Big Jo Jo's face, I suddenly realize I cannot see him nearly so well.

A heavy fog has come up.

"Ah," says Big Jo Jo, "ah, ah, ah. It is much better now."

We wait a while longer and the fog gets thicker so that we cannot see the moon and the night becomes almost black. We cannot see the dike at all.

I know that fogs sometimes come up very suddenly in the dike country of Slovakia, especially at this time of the year. However, it is true that the Lord parted the Red Sea too.

Now we get ready for our try at the dike. Big Jo Jo whispers to us, "Form into a line." He crawls up and down our line to give us final instructions.

"From here on, on your bellies. Crawl. Keep way down. And no sound. If you can live without breathing, do not breathe. Crawl until you get to the top. Then roll over the top of the dike. Roll as fast as possible."

He stops and talks with the little children. The father will take the boy over. The mother's brother will take the girl. It is awful to think what a yell from these sweet ones will do to us all. Big Jo Jo pats them on the head.

"All right, my little ones," he says solemnly. "Be good now."

Then he says to us all, "Now we go."

Big Jo Jo stays ahead of us, and when he motions we stop. We crawl and stop, crawl and stop at his signal. He signals with both hands, and in one hand I can see that he is carrying his pistol.

On all fours, all nineteen of us go up the dike bank.

It slants up for six or seven feet. Then comes the top, which is ten feet across, and we roll over it. Then it is six or seven more feet down the bank on the other side, and we go tumbling, scrambling down.

The little ones, praise the Holy Savior, never whimper.

On the other side Big Jo Jo crawls fast and we go very fast after him into a woods. Here we rest a moment. He whispers to me.

"How goes it, Sister?"

My heart is thundering; I know he must hear it. "It goes with God's help, Big Jo Jo."

"With God's help," he repeats. "Tell God the worst of it is over."

We go on quickly, through trees now instead of open fields. And soon we come to the Morava River.

It is an uncertain river, sometimes swollen, sometimes quiet, and always muddy but now, bless St. Joseph, quiet. Little Jo Jo pumps up the rubber boat. Then Big Jo Jo takes the family over the river, paddling and paying out the clothesline as he goes. Then we pull the boat back with the rope, and four by four we go over the river, being pulled now instead of paddling. I am in the last load, with Little Jo Jo and two students. I get out of the rubber boat and for the first time in my life I stand on strange soil.

I look across at my own land. I cannot even see it because of the fog.

We are much safer now, though there is still some danger. After a long walk we come to a house owned by a member of the Underground. Here we clean off the mud from the fields and the dike, and then we take a train. We reach Vienna at dawn. We cross into the U.S. zone of Vienna on a streetcar, and go to a convent. Big Jo Jo turns us over to a priest and tells us goodbye.

"Sir, may God reward you, Big Jo Jo," I say. I feel that I will cry.

He makes a slight bow and the corners of his mouth smile a little. "Good luck, Sister," he says. Then he is gone.

(Just a week ago I received a letter telling me that Big Jo Jo was killed trying to cross the border. It was a few days before Christmas.)

Our new leader, the Austrian priest, takes us by train to Amstetten and by bus to a high hill near the border of the U.S. zone. We walk over the hill and get on another bus to Linz.

Then we are walking up a path to a convent. The door opens and a priest stands there. The Austrian priest says, "I bring you guests again—from Slovakia."

The priest throws wide his arms. He speaks in Slovakian, for he is a Slovakian refugee himself.

"Welcome in God's name! Now you are completely free."

The Austrian priest points to me. "She's a sister."

The Slovakian priest looks and laughs. "Is that what nuns wear in Slovakia these days?"

Two weeks later I take a bus, alone, to a convent of my order at Obernzell in Bavaria. The convent is on a high hillside, and I walk up the ninety-two steps. I ring a bell. A sister opens a peephole in the door and asks, "What do you want?"

"I am Sister Cecilia," I say. "Of the Daughters of the Most Holy Savior."

The sister studies me carefully and snaps the peephole shut. Through the door I can hear her talking to the Mother Superior over a telephone.

"There is a lady out here in secular clothes," she says. "She claims she is a sister. I wonder if she isn't out of her mind. She is wearing pants."

The Mother Superior herself comes to the door. She looks at me and I at her and suddenly we recognize each other. Once she visited our convent in Bratislava and I sang a German song for her, a song about the "Heavenly Fields."

The Mother Superior smiles broadly and opens the door. "Welcome, Sister," she says. "Come into the Heavenly Fields."

Once I am inside the convent the first thing I do is ask, "Mother Superior, may I have a nun's habit?"

The sisters, who have come running to see me, now bring me all the parts of our habit. Soon I am again properly dressed.

As they take me down the hall, we walk through the dining room. Suddenly I stop, for I think I see someone I know. Then it comes to me that I am looking at the polished door of a dish cupboard. I realize it is myself I see, Sister Cecilia. I stop and look and look and look—though I know you are not supposed to look, forgive me, St. Joseph. I look like myself.

*   *   *

After Sister Cecilia came to the United States, she entered the convent of her order at the Holy Redeemer College in Oakland, California.

13

Hungarian Refugees

At a mass meeting in Castle Garden in New York City, several thousand people had gathered to welcome Lajos Kossuth. In the wave of revolutions that swept through Europe in 1848, he had been the leader in the movement to free Hungary from the rule of the Austrian house of Hapsburg. The revolt might well have succeeded, had not the Hapsburg emperor called on the Russian czar for help, and Russian troops were used to put down the rebellion. Kossuth took refuge in Turkey, and from there he wrote an open letter to the American people. What the Hungarians had wanted, he explained, was a chance to rule themselves.

This statement aroused sympathy in a nation that had fought for its own independence three quarters of a century earlier, and he was invited to visit the United States. The speech of Castle Garden was the first of many that he was to give. His audiences wept and cheered, and even Daniel Webster, the dignified Secretary of State, was swept up by the enthusiasm. At one banquet he proposed a toast to "Hungarian independence, Hungarian self-government, Hungarian control of Hungarian destinies."

The United States government, though, did not offer the military aid that Kossuth had hoped for, and he sailed for England a disappointed man. But many of the soldiers who had fought beside him and then fled to America when their revolt failed stayed on to become American citizens. Passionately devoted to the cause of liberty, about eight hundred of them volunteered to serve in the Union Army during the Civil War and several were commissioned generals.

Nearly a century later the United States was to welcome many

151

more refugees from Hungary. In the intervening years much had happened to their native land. In 1867 it became an equal partner in the Austro-Hungarian Empire, with the Austrian emperor also acting as king of Hungary. The empire was broken up, after its defeat in World War I, and for a few months Hungary was a republic before Communists took over the government. During World War II the country was occupied in turn by the Nazis and by troops from the Soviet Union. In the late 1940s Hungary was proclaimed a so-called "People's Republic" in the Soviet bloc, and the new generation growing up was indoctrinated with Communist ideas at school

At home, though, many parents secretly instructed their children in the true history of their country. They memorized the poems of the national poet, Sandor Petöfi, who had been killed in the 1848 revolution. One favorite began with the words:

> *Arise, Hungarians, the Fatherland calls you.*
> *The time is now! Now or never!*
> *Live oppressed—or live in freedom,*
> *That is the question to be decided.*

The lines of that poem may well have inspired some of the young people who sparked the uprising of October, 1956. It started as a peaceful demonstration when university students, some of whom still considered themselves loyal Communists, gathered before the radio building in Budapest. They wanted to broadcast their demands for more freedom from a government that was dominated by the Soviet Union, but the AVO, the secret police who guarded the station, opened fire on the demonstrators.

The students fought back, and for two weeks the streets of Budapest were a battlefield. The majority of the freedom fighters were young, but older workers also joined in the struggle. They had no weapons except rifles and homemade bombs, but the authorities were alarmed. They agreed to satisfy some of the students' demands, and for five wonderful days they were convinced that they had won some measure of liberty for their country.

They found out their mistake when Soviet forces from Russia arrived with tanks and armored cars to put down the rebellion. Many freedom fighters were slaughtered, others imprisoned. Still others were rounded up and loaded into boxcars to be deported to work camps in the Soviet Union. A cry for help was broadcast from a radio station in Budapest: "The shadows grow darker every hour over the soil of Hungary. Listen to our cry, civilized people of the world, and act. Extend us your fraternal aid."

Shocked though many people were in Western Europe and in America, to send military aid to the freedom fighters would have meant violating the territory of the countries that surrounded Hungary. What the free world could and did do was to help the refugees who escaped. Of the 200,000 who left during those perilous days, the majority went first to Austria. They were cared for in hastily set up refugee centers by workers in volunteer organizations. Some of the escapees remained in Austria, but arrangements were made for many others to travel to new homes scattered throughout the world. The largest number—36,000—went to Canada. Almost as many were flown to the United States, where they stayed at Camp Kilmer in New Jersey until housing and jobs could be found for them elsewhere.

Not all of the newcomers were able to find employment in the fields for which they had been trained. Lawyers sometimes washed dishes to make a living for their families. A former army officer became a janitor. An architect had to be satisfied with an unskilled job in a factory. Others, more fortunate, found positions that made use of the skills they had developed in their native land. Two boys who escaped with their parents in 1956 grew up to be professional football players. They were Pete and Charlie Gogolak.

Another refugee, whose name has been honored both in the United States and in Hungary, was Jozsef Kovago, a former soldier and engineer. During some of the most troubled years of his country's history, he had resisted the totalitarian regimes of both Nazis and Communists. At the age of thirty-seven he was elected mayor of Budapest in that city's last free election, but after the Communists gained control he was imprisoned for six years by the AVO. He was released a few months before the uprising of 1956, but after Soviet tanks put down the rebellion his name was again on the AVO's list of most wanted men. It was a difficult decision to leave the city he loved, but his arrest was imminent, and he realized that he would probably be executed as so many other patriots had been. On November 20, 1956, he and his wife, Lonci, and their little daughter, Catherine, boarded a train that was to carry them on the first lap of their long journey toward the West.

The following selection is from Mr. Kovago's book, *You Are All Alone.*

Out of Darkness (1956)

BY JOZSEF KOVAGO

The crowded train rattled toward Austria; somehow people settled themselves, the women and children found places on the floor or on knapsacks. We tried to guess about the future and wondered whether the AVO would search the train.

I overheard some railroad men talking at one station platform. A big red-nosed man said, "This crowd will finally land in Siberia." His reference, of course, was to the possibility that we would be captured at the border. I glanced at my wife, Lonci. She was pale and frightened, but the awkwardness of the situation was relieved by a man standing next to me who sensed the tension. . . .

"Don't worry. All the railroad men are with the refugees. They all want to help you," he said.

The railroad men were looking out for the AVO, someone explained. They tried to time the arrival of the train so it wouldn't coincide with the presence of the dreaded authorities at the station.

Suddenly a tall man next to me, who had not spoken before, turned to me.

"You don't know me. But I know who you are and that's enough. My task is to accompany you to the border. I will take care of all of you. Later on, we will move to the engine. You and your family will be hidden there. Even if the AVO men search the train, they won't find you."

"Thank you very much," I whispered.

"Don't mention it."

He was off, trying to get some water for Catherine, our little girl.

In a whisper I explained all this to Lonci, trying to put her mind at rest. About an hour later, when we reached the station at Tata, I noticed our tall friend deeply engaged in conversation with some railroad men on the platform. After a few minutes he came up to me.

He talked to me in a low voice. "The AVO plans to search the train at Gyor, asking everybody for identification. The train will go as fast as it can to get to the station before the patrol, if it's possible. The railroad men are keeping in touch with one another, trying to time the schedule accordingly." Should this scheme fail, however, I could always use his identification papers. He had a legal permit to go to the Austrian border to purchase some lumber, he told me.

"How about you?" I said. "What will happen to you?"

"I will just tell them about my relatives living close by. Don't worry about me. All you have to look out for is getting through safely."

In a few minutes' time the train stopped. The tall man came up to me, pressed his identification card in my hand, and took us up to the engine. There were two narrow pathways on the engine; that's where we were hidden. It was far from being a deluxe trip. We squatted most of the way, every minute a minute nearer to freedom.

Nearing the Gyor station, we were warned not to talk but to lie flat on our stomachs. The engineer told us that, according to rumors, an especially strong Russian patrol, combined with an AVO detachment, was going to search the train. The train stopped and we felt the anxiety of every minute. Each seemed like hours. Finally the train started to move with a jerk. The engineer was happy. He said I could stand up, and he took me to the controls.

"Look out there," he said, pointing to the window. "We sure pulled a fast one on them."

We saw two Russian tanks and an AVO detachment. The men were armed with submachine guns. There must have been about fifteen or twenty of them. They waved their arms, trying to halt the train. Our friend the engineer put on full steam, and the train started racing as never before.

I was relieved. I felt that there was only one more thing to worry about, and that was crossing the border.

Around three o'clock in the afternoon the train slowed down on the open track and stopped. As if from nowhere my tall friend appeared, helping us with the knapsack and explaining, "We can't go on. The next station is full of AVO men and Russkis. You'll have to start from here."

I shook his hand and tried to express our gratitude.

"Forget it," he said. "I hope God will help you to reach our friends abroad and shake up their consciences. I hope you will return to us soon."

With this we parted. The rest of the passengers, about two or three hundred people, also alighted from the train. Now we had to head for the fields. What followed was "operation mud." Going through the wet fields, our city shoes stuck deep in the mud at every step. They were certainly not made for this sort of excursion.

The crowd broke up into small groups. I would have liked to join one group which moved fast. Their leader obviously knew the area. However, my friend's wife had come with us from Budapest, and I had to help her get through the tortuous path. We must have gone about a mile or so when we heard shots fired in front of us. In a few minutes we reached a railroad crossing. A railroad man was standing there with a bicycle.

"Turn around, all of you; you are running into a trap!" he shouted. "Don't you see that the forward group has been captured by the Russians? Lie down flat; the Russkis will be here in a minute."

I disregarded his warning, gripped Lonci's and Catherine's hands, and pulled them over the rails. Then I helped my

friend's wife. We ran as fast as we could on the other side of
the track at a distance from the rest of the group, hoping that
we would not be conspicuous. We still heard the railroad man
shouting, warning the others. Then he came over to us.

"Come along with me," he said. "You can hide at my house."

A few hundred yards ahead of us was a small house. It must
have belonged to the railroad watchman. Several haystacks
stood near the house. When we got there the place was
crowded with refugees. The watchman and his wife gave us all
hot tea and tried to make us comfortable. More and more
people arrived. The watchman hid the newcomers in the haystacks. I struck up a conversation with him. I offered him
money if he could get us someone to guide us across the border.

"Stay here for the night," he said. "We'll see what happens
tomorrow."

We took off our shoes and started eating some of the food
from our knapsacks. Lonci had a terrible headache. I made her
lie down on the bed. Catherine was excited and thoroughly
enjoyed the situation.

"Look, Daddy," she exclaimed, "the stars are falling."

I glanced out the window. The Russians were firing rockets,
which lit up the whole area. Every time one went up its ghost-
like color penetrated the room we sat in. From a distance we
heard the rumbling of tanks. We felt tired and frightened.

Suddenly I heard men arriving in front and the clatter of
guns. My military training immediately helped me to identify
the noise. I could not be mistaken. "So that's it," I said. "The
railroad man set a trap for us. It's the patrol arriving now."

I looked around the room; the watchman was gone.

"What is it?" Lonci asked in a frightened whisper.

"Just some guide, I guess, the one our host spoke about."

Lonci pressed her hand into mine and whispered, "These
are soldiers. They've come to arrest us."

"Wait. We're not sure yet," I said. I grabbed my pocket knife and the big torchlight. It might be a hand-to-hand fight. I wouldn't sell myself cheaply. I hadn't fought for years, but if necessary I wouldn't hesitate to do my best. Everyone in the room was silent. There was a strong tension in the air. Then we heard the voice of the railroad man from the outside.

"Stay, friends, for a cup of tea. Don't bother about those unfortunate refugees. They are Hungarians too. We all have these Russkis on our necks."

"Well, that's true for sure," another voice answered. "In any case, nothing can happen at night. They can't start for the border now."

Slowly I walked to the door, opened it a little, and looked out. There were six soldiers sitting outside. I sighed, relieved. They were Hungarian regular soldiers whose sympathy was with the refugees. They spoke about the reinforced Soviet units patrolling the whole border area. The Russians had sent up the rockets. They had also captured about a hundred and fifty refugees that afternoon and evening.

No, the soldiers didn't think we should start now. They would stay with us for a while, and then they would go on as if they hadn't seen us at all. Our host walked by and I grabbed him.

"What's going on?" I asked.

"The soldiers will leave," he whispered. "Then around nine o'clock two guides will come and take you to a farm. You will all go there and stay until it's safe to start for the border. Don't worry. Everyone is keeping a watch on the Russians."

Around nine o'clock the soldiers said farewell. "Good luck," they told us before they left. The first guide arrived a few minutes later, and fifteen of us started out in the group.

It was an icy cold night. The mud froze on our shoes. We were bitter, tired, and desperate. The one exception was Catherine. She enjoyed every minute of this strange excursion. To her it was a game. The man in the front lay down and the others followed suit. No one would scold her for muddying her coat. It was a splendid game, she thought. Lonci was less enthusiastic. She was worried lest Chatherine catch cold. Whenever we lay down in the mud she tried to pull the child to herself, so she wouldn't get too wet.

Finally, we spied some lights in the distance. After another weary walk we arrived at the farm. It was a wonderful feeling to be in a warm room once again. The place was full of people, most of them refugees. Two farm girls were sleeping in beds; the rest of us lay down on the floor using our overcoats as a bed.

The guide told us that we could start after midnight. He suggested that we try to sleep and get some energy. Then he turned on the radio. Radio Free Europe broadcasts throughout the night, and it provided good information about the Soviet troops which guarded the border.

I tried to comfort Lonci and Catherine. I did my best to tell them some jokes, rubbing their limbs to warm them. Catherine was impatient; she wanted to start right away.

"Where are we going, Daddy?" she asked.

"We are going to Austria, dear," I answered.

"There are no Russkis there, are there?" she inquired. "And no one wants to put you in prison there. Right?" she persisted.

"That's right, my dear. Austria is in the free world."

"Why can't Hungary be free too?" she said. "I wish she were."

I didn't quite know how to answer that question.

After midnight we started out on the most difficult part of our journey. We had ten miles ahead of us, through cornfields, half-frozen mud, woods, and irrigation ditches. The icy wind chilled us to the bone. It seemed to be an endless journey in the darkness. Every step meant an effort to disengage our feet from the heavy clay and put them falteringly forward. The whole world disappeared in the darkness. We were a small piece of isolated humanity trying to find its way from the known terror into the unknown wilderness.

We were tired beyond feeling. Our legs were numb. The

knapsack straps bit into our shoulders. I never knew that a small sack could be that heavy. The darkness was broken occasionally by searchlights. This meant that we were pursued and gave us added impetus to move again. Every time the light came near, we lay down in the mud and listened to our pounding hearts. It took a superhuman effort to get up again. The journey went on endlessly.

The light gray shadow of a road caused our guides to stop. They motioned us to be quiet and listened to the sounds in the night.

I heard them whispering. "Maybe we will make it in time," one of them said.

"Don't you think it better to wait?" the other one inquired.

"The Russian patrol will come the same way. If we stay they'll get us," the first one said. "If we start and run fast we have a chance."

"Let's go," he said.

We crossed the highway. About two hundred yards beyond it we heard the rumble of tanks.

"Lie down flat," our guide ordered us.

A rocket streaked skyward, lighting up the whole countryside. We hugged the ground, trying to melt into the freezing mud. The tanks rumbled by close to us and fired shots at random along the road. The searchlight swung round and round, barely missing our little group. Lonci grabbed Catherine and buried her head under her coat. We waited, terror-stricken, but the tanks kept on going. Soon their rumble died in the distance. We jumped up and started to run, gathering all our strength for this final spurt.

The guide kept saying; "Keep on . . . we are very close now. . . ."

In minutes we reached a bare, open area like a half-completed highway. The grass was cut on a strip of land about six yards wide. The ground was smooth. The guides stopped us and told us that this was the border. Here they said goodbye and told us to head straight for the dim lights in the distance. That was the first Austrian village. We should be very careful to go straight on with no wavering, for the border line zigzagged here, and if we were not careful we might yet land in the arms of a Russian patrol.

"Good luck to you in the free world," they said, and disappeared in the night.

Almost instinctively I crouched down and picked up a piece of earth—the earth of the Motherland. Then I threw it away. There was plenty on my shoes, I thought, and besides my heart was filled with it, filled with the strange mixture of smiles, tears, friends, houses, rivers, hills, birds, trees, and even prisons, all of which combined to make up one's Motherland. I looked back for a final view of this land I loved so much and had suffered so much for, trying to find in this last glimpse a symbol to carry away with me. There was nothing but darkness.

Then suddenly I saw a shimmering light in the distance. I do not know what it was, but it gave me the symbol I was searching for. In the oppressive darkness the flickering of a spark which cannot be extinguished and burns forever like the torch of freedom and eternal hope.

*　　*　　*

After several more exhausting hours the refugees reached an Austrian village where they were cared for by the Austrian Red Cross. But Jozsef Kovago was anxious to be on his way, convinced that he had a mission. He wanted to urge capital cities in the Free World to declare their solidarity with Budapest and—when Hungary was free again—to furnish the funds to help rebuild the shattered city.

In Vienna he met members of the International Rescue Committee, an organization sponsored by private American citizens. Through this organization he was enabled to visit The Hague and London and finally to come to the United States. On January 28, 1957, he stood before the United Nations Special Committee to report on the Hungarian tragedy. Later he went on goodwill tours of South America and the Far East before returning to a new home he had made for his family in a quiet suburban community in New Jersey.

In the United States Mr. Kovago has resumed his work as a mechanical engineer and has been honored with the Freedom Award, at Freedom House in New York City, and an honorary degree from Bard College. In the list of honors he was requested to name, he included the fact that he became an American citizen in 1968.

14

Exiles from Spain

Among the early refugees to reach the region that is now the United States were the Sephardic Jews—those whose ancestors had lived in Spain or Portugal. As a result of the Spanish Inquisition, the Jews had been expelled from Spain the same year Columbus had discovered America, but they were forced to leave their wealth behind to enrich the royal treasury. Some of the Marranos, those Jews who had embraced or pretended to embrace the Catholic faith, joined their friends in their wanderings from place to place, trying to find a country where they would be safe.

A number of their descendants eventually settled in the Portuguese colony of Brazil, but here too the Inquisition made life perilous for them, and in 1654, twenty-three Sephardic refugees arrived in New Amsterdam, later to become New York. The ship they had chartered to carry them to the Netherlands had been attacked by Spaniards. The Jews on board would have perished had not the captain of a French ship rescued them and brought them to the little Dutch colony.

They were a sad-looking group without money and with only the clothes they were wearing. Peter Stuyvesant, the hot-tempered governor, was as intolerant in his way as the Spanish and Brazilian Catholics were in theirs, and he wanted no one in his colony except members of the Dutch Reformed Church. He ordered the Jews to leave, but he did not have the last word. In Holland, the directors of the Dutch West Indies Company that managed the colony were anxious to attract new settlers. The governor was ordered to "let everyone remain free as long as he does not offend others or oppose the government."

Other Jews of Spanish ancestry arrived and continued to live in the

163

colony after it was taken over by the English and renamed New York. They also settled in Philadelphia, Charleston, and other towns. Altogether, about two thousand Jews were living in the colonies by the time the American Revolution began. Many of the men fought under General Washington. After he became President of the new country, he received a letter of congratulation from the congregation of the synagogue in Newport, Rhode Island. The members wanted to express their gratitude for "a government that gives . . . no assistance to persecution but affords to all liberty of conscience."

For a long time other people of Spanish descent had been living in the region later to become the southwest part of the United States. The land of their ancestors was not the powerful nation it had once been. As the years passed, the masses of poor people in Spain seemed to become even poorer. Finally in 1931, because of popular discontent under his rule, King Alfonso XIII was forced into exile. An election was held, and a majority of the voters chose to make Spain a republic.

It was not a united republic. The new government tried to introduce needed reforms but was opposed by forces of both the extreme Right and the extreme Left. A bloody civil war followed between the rebel army under the command of Francisco Franco and the Loyalists who were determined to preserve the republic. By 1936 the rebel forces, with decisive aid from Nazi Germany and Fascist Italy, finally won, and Franco became president and dictator of Spain.

Among those who realized what was going to happen and decided to go into voluntary exile rather than live under a fascist regime was Juan Ramón Jiménez. He was regarded as the greatest poet of the Spanish-speaking world and was widely acclaimed when he and his wife traveled through South and Central America. In 1947 he accepted the invitation of the University of Maryland to be a visiting professor and later joined the faculty of the University of Puerto Rico. In 1956 he was awarded the Nobel Prize for literature.

Other Loyalists waited too long to leave Spain. Franco was ruthless in his treatment of those who had opposed him, and about half a million refugees fled across the snow-covered Pyrenees into southern France. In their haste to escape they abandoned their possessions and lived in hastily set up camps. During World War II many fought with the Allies or helped in the French Resistance. Some were forced into Nazi labor battalions and died. Even when the war was over, those who survived dared not return to their native land for fear of reprisals from Franco's government.

The most eloquent spokesman for these homeless ones was Pablo Casals, conductor, composer, and one of the world's great cellists. Born in the Spanish province of Catalonia in 1876, he was already world famous by the turn of the century. Though his first love was for his own province, he was dedicated to the cause of freedom for all men everywhere and refused to play in any country with an oppressive government. When the Spanish Civil War broke out he chose exile, first in the French village of Prades and later in the American commonwealth of Puerto Rico. After the war was over he was urged to return to Spain, but that he refused to do until the people could have a government of their own choice.

Instead he has enriched America with his music and the shining example of a man dedicated to an ideal. In 1957 he inaugurated the annual Festival Casals in San Juan, the capital of Puerto Rico. Later, he visited the mainland to give concerts at the United Nations and the White House. Still a voluntary exile from Spain, he decided to make his home on the beautiful island that had been his mother's birthplace.

The following selection is from the book *Conversations With Casals,* by a longtime friend. The friend's questions are in *italics,* the musician's replies in regular type.

Conversation with Pablo Casals (1957)

BY J. MARIA CORREDOR, TRANSLATED BY ANDRE MANGEOT

Is it a long time since you went to play in Russia for the last time?

Yes, I have spoken to you about my great friend Siloti, who

was the beloved disciple of Lizst. He devoted all his talent and work to the cause of popular education, and by so doing raised the mental standards of the people. He and a few friends subsidized an important orchestra which gave concerts for the students and workers. He lived for his art and for the people. The most eminent Russian musicians met at his house.

Then came the October Revolution [of 1918], when everything was taken from him and he was subjected to all the usual inquisitions and interrogations. He became ill; as a living place for his wife and five children he was given the kitchen of his own house and a small adjacent room. The rest of his house was occupied by young men of the new regime, and in order to survive, Siloti and his family had to do the most impossible and degrading things. The only valuable they managed to hide was a necklace. And it was thanks to the value of this that after two or three years of martyrdom they managed to escape to Finland.

I was very worried about them, since I did not receive any news. But one day, I received a letter from Antwerp from Siloti saying, "We are here." I went off immediately, and when I met them at Antwerp I could hardly recognize them; they looked like ghosts. Since that day I have never wanted to go back to Russia. I do realize that in a revolution certain excesses unfortunately cannot be avoided; but I don't accept that, under the pretext of forming a new social order, these leaders think they can persecute blindly the very people who have practiced fraternity with the workers and the people. The end does not justify the means. I have protested and always shall protest against inhuman means.

And a few years later we had the Nazis who began persecuting people. . . .

Ah . . . when I saw that Einstein, Thomas Mann, Bruno Walter, and so many illustrious personalities of science and the arts had to expatriate themselves, some persecuted because of their race, others because of their ideas, I thought it was my duty to protest, and I declared I would not go back to Germany until intellectual and artistic liberties were restored. When, later on, Mussolini imitated the Nazis, I adopted the same attitude toward Italy. The only weapons I possess are the cello and the conductor's baton. They are not very deadly, but I have no others. In the circumstances I used what I had to protest against what I considered was disgraceful and ig-nominious.

However, the German public had a great veneration for you.

It was very painful to leave them, but I thought that by taking this attitude I was more faithful to Bach and Beethoven, and all they stood for, than to the people who through weak-ness or fanaticism soiled the honor of a great country.

This attitude, and the one you took later, have raised a lot of comment on the subject of the relation between art and politics.

I am not a politician. But the question is whether art is to be a pastime or toy for men to play with, or if it should have a deep and human meaning. An artist, to my mind, is under obligation to take sides, whatever sacrifice it means, if human dignity becomes involved. When I see innocent blood spilled and the tears of the victims of injustice, they become more important to me than my music.

In the course of the first and terrible phase of the Spanish tragedy, I got so indignant one day that I did not hesitate to risk my life to save a man who was persecuted. I was at Sant Salvador practicing the cello. Two armed men entered my room and said, "We have been told that Mr. X is here." (He was a businessman from Barcelona who spent the summer in a house next to mine.)

"He is not here," I said.

They went off. A moment later they returned with poor Mr. X, whom they had arrested and who already feared the worst; his wife was at his side crying. "We know you have a telephone and we want to telephone to Vendrell to get them to send a cart." (Those famous carts they used for carrying condemned people to be shot.)

I faced them and said, "I shall do the telephoning, not you. Why did you arrest this man? You will not take Mr. X away, do you hear?"

They had revolvers and guns. I had nothing; but the tone of my voice made them understand that I meant what I said. They had a moment of hesitation which was decisive. They muttered, "We had orders from the mayor of Vendrell."

I took the telephone and talked to the man who was supposed to be the mayor. My words were of such a kind that he got frightened and said, "These men have made a mistake. I told them to go somewhere else." The tone of his voice belied his words. I communicated his answer to the men and told them they could go and that Mr. X would stay. As they went through the door they gave me a look of hatred and threatened me as well.

It shows that you had taken a stand.

Yes. For me and most of the Spanish intellectuals it was a question of principle. The main responsibility for the civil war fell on those who tried to abolish by force a legitimate government (which had been elected by popular votes a few months before.) And when their *pronunciamento* failed, they tried to secure the help of Fascist Italy and Nazi Germany. In all civilized countries one should accept the decision of the people, and those who are not satisfied should wait for the next elections.

The Barcelona University bestowed on you the title of Doctor honoris causa *in rather strange circumstances.*

Very strange, when you think that the authorities of the Academy signed the diploma the day before Franco's army came into Barcelona! That was the last meeting of the university. Even then Italian planes were flying over the town all the time; evacuation had already started. Yet, at a time as painful and critical as it was, my country thought of paying me such a moving tribute. I shall never forget it.

When the civil war ended, did you decide to live in Prades immediately?

No. I had been away a little while, playing at concerts, and when the war ended I was in Paris. I felt broken and worn out. The news I got from home was terrible: oppression had begun in Catalonia; thousands of refugees were in concentration camps in the south of France; my house in Sant Salvador was occupied and ransacked by the Franco troops; my brother Luis was maltreated because he was my brother. . . . His situation obsessed me. He had such a fine character. A friend from Barcelona came to see me in Paris. He was the first person who told me about Prades, where he had been a resident. He said it was a pretty little town at the foot of the Canigou, where almost everyone talks Catalan. This got me out of my torpor, and I decided to go and live in Prades.

Did you enjoy your stay?

As soon as I got there the landscape, so much like that of Catalonia, acted on me like a sedative.

You had some hard work in front of you?

I gave myself up to relieving my unfortunate compatriots who were living in camps close by. Some Catalan friends, exiled in Prades also, helped me to organize everything. I took a room in an hotel where we set up a regular office to centralize all the gifts, the purchases, the demands and distribution. We had lorries loaded with food and garments going to the camps. I wrote to friends for funds and we were glad of any gifts.

You visited the camps pretty often?

Yes, and the camps were frightful, not because of deliberate cruelty but because of the confusion which had prevailed when they were established. The unfortunate people who were shut up there lacked the most elementary commodities. I realized that my visits brought some consolation to those who had lost contact with the world outside. I tried to send small gifts to all those who asked me, and wrote lit-

tle notes of encouragement. In those days I wrote thousands
of letters and postcards.

*The Second World War had started. Did you expect any
danger?*

Yes, I did. And my friends abroad even more. I received so
many letters from American friends advising me to leave
Europe and come to them.

*To be exiled in America, sheltered from all danger, and also
able to make a fortune with playing. . . .*

No, I could not do that. My duty was to stay with my compatriots who, like myself, had been hunted from their country,
and try to comfort them with my presence.

*When the French defeat came in June, 1940, you must have
found yourself in a difficult position.*

Very. At that time I thought all was lost in Europe. Also the
rumor was spreading that the Spanish army, taking advantage
of the French retreat, would cross the Pyrenees. Some refugee
friends and I hired two cars to go to Bordeaux, in the hope of
sailing to England from there. Before leaving I had burnt all
the compromising papers I had, to save my correspondents
from pursuit. (How I regretted the destruction of thousands of
letters I had received from the camps. They formed a human
document of such extraordinary interest.)

When we reached Bordeaux we heard that the ship we
hoped to sail in had been sunk by the German air force the day
before. We tried other ships but it was all impossible. We had
to return to Prades, which we reached after a very difficult
journey as all the roads were filled with refugees. There was
such a panic at the time that when we got back to our hotel
at Prades, in the middle of the night, no one would open the
door. It was only because the tobacconist opposite heard us
and let us in that we did not spend the night outside.

After that I went to live in the Villa Colette for a few years.
I went on with the work of helping my compatriots in the
camps.

Did you continue to give concerts during these years?

Before and after June, 1940, I went to Switzerland in order to get the necessary funds to live on. When the French armistice was signed I thought I ought to help the French, who were going through a very difficult time. I gave concerts for charity in the free zone. But after the Allied landing in North Africa the whole of France was occupied. I would not leave Prades, and with the German troops everywhere I thought silence was the only possible attitude.

Did the Germans worry you?

Once some agents of the Gestapo came to the Villa Colette and went through every bit of paper I had and when they retired said, "Be careful. If our suspicions are confirmed we will arrest you."

The atmosphere became more and more intolerable. One day from my room window I saw three German officers coming through the gate and I thought we were in for it. They came in, behaved extremely well, and said, after a military salute, "We are great admirers of yours and we have come to greet you and find out how you are."

They sat down and started a conversation which lasted over two hours. "So you are the Casals our fathers and grandfathers told us about?"

"I am."

After a series of praises they came to the usual question: "And why don't you go and play in Germany?"

"For the same reason I do not go and play in Spain."

"Wouldn't you like to come and play in Berlin again? Hitler himself will come and hear you, and if you like we'll put a railway carriage at your disposal."

"No, thank you."

I guessed they wanted me to play to them, but I was determined I would not do it. So when they asked me to take my cello, I told them I had had rheumatic pains in the shoulder for some days and could not play. They saw my instrument and plucked the strings. I felt disturbed at the thought that perhaps these hands had spilled blood or were tainted.

"Is this the cello you played on in Germany?"

"Very often."

The Commandant sat at the piano and started a Bach aria to get me going . . . it was useless.

"We cannot go away without a souvenir from you."

I understood their chief would ask them for proof of their visit; I signed a photograph on which I wrote, "In remembrance of your visit to Prades." As they went, and I looked out of the window, they asked me if they could take a photograph (another proof). I did not see them again. But I had not played for them.

After the Allied landing in Normandy, the situation must have been even more tense.

Yes. A young man who was engaged to the daughter of a friend of mine, and who had joined the "French Militia" so that he would not be sent to Germany, told me he had seen my name on a list of people who were to be arrested. He had heard the local chief say, "When the time comes, Casals will see what is in store for him." This young man had the courage to stand up to him and said it was infamous and that he would lodge a protest in front of anyone concerned.

For some reason we were left at liberty after the landing took place in Normandy. During those days every hour seemed like a hundred years. There was a moment of great danger: the Maquis [the French Underground] operating in the Pyrenees came to Prades and attacked the house where the Gestapo was operating. One German got killed and many were wounded. What would be the reprisals? We could have been shot. Fortunately the mayor of Prades went to the military commander and told him all the responsibility for the attack should be his. Nothing happened, and shortly afterward the moment we had been hoping for arrived. The German troops, when they knew the Allies were winning, evacuated the town. The French were once more in control, and hope became a reality. Our exile (at least so we thought) was nearing its end.

Two weeks later the young man of the Militia, of whom I have spoken, was on trial with three others [for collaborating with the enemy]. I was summoned as a witness after I had written to the president of the Tribunal to explain what he had done for me. The atmosphere of the court was thick with excitement and hatred for this Militia. I was feeling sick with fear for the life of the young man. I stuck to what I had said in my letter. Out of the four accused, three were given the death penalty and executed; the fourth, my young friend, was given thirty years' solitary confinement, but he only stayed in prison two or three years and was released.

You probably saved his life.

He had probably saved mine first. In any case, in those horrible days it was a small comfort to have been able to save one human life.

After the liberation you must have felt you were morally free to start playing again. I know you then received quantities of invitations. Everywhere they thought of you as a great artist who had resisted the seductions as well as the threats of Hitler.

After my voluntary banishment during those years, I started playing abroad again in the hope that I should soon be able to go back to my country as a free citizen. I went to England twice, to Switzerland, and also gave concerts in Paris and other French towns. Unfortunately the duration of this tour was much shorter than I had anticipated.

When you were in Switzerland you received a visit from Don Juan de Bourbon, the pretender to the Spanish throne?

Yes, and when we began to talk, this grandson of Queen Maria Cristina told me how often his father and grandmother had spoken to him about me. He was very affectionate.

Did he talk to you about Spanish politics?

He asked me what I thought of the Spanish situation and I

gave him my sincere opinion. I said that I would not be a party
to either a republic or a monarchy, but I would accept the
regime freely chosen by my country. My adherence to this
regime would depend on what it did, not on its label.

What was your impression of the Pretender?

He seemed full of sincerity and goodwill. He agreed that a
national plebiscite should decide the form of the future regime
of Spain, and he added that he did not feel inclined to accept
any direct offer made by the dictator [Franco]. But later on,
Don Juan changed his mind. He no longer contemplated a
national plebiscite to find out what the Spanish people wanted,
and he agreed that his eldest son should be brought up in Spain
under the auspices of the dictatorial government. So it looks as
if Don Juan just obeyed the law of the dictator, and he is not
the only one; the governments of most democratic nations
have done the same.

*   *   *

Don Pablo came to this conclusion in 1947 during a concert tour
in England. He was bitterly disappointed that the British government, as well as that of the United States, had refused to take a stand
against the Franco regime. It was not right, he declared, that he
accept acclaim and large fees when so many of his countrymen were
still in exile. Returning to Prades he announced that he would accept
no more engagements "as long as Spain still lacks a government
which respects the fundamental liberties and the will of the people."

During the next few years only his pupils and a few friends heard
him play. In 1950 he was persuaded to take part in a music festival
honoring the two hundredth birthday of Johann Sebastian Bach. It
was so successful that the festival became an annual event, as did the
one he later inaugurated in Puerto Rico.

An old hope was revived. Perhaps through his music Don Pablo
could help to bring closer the day for which he longed—the day, he
once said, "when the peoples of the world will sit down together
bound by love and happiness, as in one great concert hall."

15

Refugees from the Chinese Mainland

Two Chinas were the unfortunate result of a bitter civil war that ravaged that country. In 1949 the forces of Nationalist China were driven from the mainland to set up a rival government on the island of Taiwan (called Formosa by the Portuguese), about a hundred miles to the east. Since then the Communists have been in control of the mainland, which they named the People's Republic of China. It has more than 760 million inhabitants. Some of the thousands who escaped after 1949 have told graphic stories of why and how they fled.

Leaving all of their possessions behind, they eluded armed guards, fought off savage dogs sent to pursue them, crawled under electrified barbed-wire fences, and crossed icy waters in leaky sampans in their desperate effort to get away. Those who succeeded in reaching the city of Hong Kong, a British colony, usually arrived without funds and in need of food, clothing, and a place to stay. The population of that city more than doubled with the influx of the refugees, most of whom built temporary shacks out of any material they could find.

One Chinese who was permitted to travel by train to Hong Kong and then had the good fortune to join relatives in the United States was a young girl named Sansan. She had been brought up as a member of the Soo family. But the man Sansan called "Papa" seemed indifferent, whereas "Mama"—perhaps because of a chronic ailment —often made life unbearable. The girl had an endless round of duties, cleaning the house, chopping wood for fuel, and getting out of bed at 3 A.M. to stand with ration card in hand in a long line of hungry people hoping to buy enough food for the day. Though undernour-

175

ished and often ill, she managed to make good grades at school. At fourteen she was assigned to another school to be trained as an elementary school teacher. Education in China was free, but when Sansan protested that she wanted to go on to college, she was given to understand that such decisions were for the government to make.

"Your wishes should be the wishes of China," she was told. "China now needs teachers for the Great Leap Forward, and you are assigned to be one of them. . . . Don't be ungrateful."

Her entire future had been decided for her, or so it seemed in 1962, when she received a letter that was to set in motion a series of events that would bring about a great change in her life. The following selection is adapted from her book, *Eighth Moon.*

I Belong to Myself (1962)

BY SANSAN, AS TOLD TO BETTE LORD

In the spring of my sixteenth year, I received a letter from Grandmother asking me to call on her as soon as possible. When I reached the house, Grandmother's youngest daughter, Goo Ma, answered my knock. She was a handsome woman with the disciplined air of the teacher that she was. She told me that Grandmother had been very ill with pneumonia and, at eighty-three, she thought it wise to see her relatives and settle all her affairs.

I was badly shaken by the news, for I loved the old woman well. She was always kind and loving. Even though I was only a distant relative, she had often teased me about being her favorite child and always remembered my birthdays and holidays with generous presents.

After Goo Ma finished her account of Grandmother's condition, she pointed to a door and said, "Mother's room has been changed. Since Grandfather's death, she doesn't need the big bedroom upstairs any more; so she has moved into the basement. Go down the stairs and you will find her in bed."

The basement room was small and lined with trunks. Grandmother was propped up with pillows on her bed, dozing, and I sat on the extra cot to wait until she finished her nap. Even sleeping, Grandmother looked neat, her white hair pulled tightly back to a small circular bun framing her ageless face. She was a tiny woman, not even five feet tall, and looked helpless with her eyes closed. As I glanced around I became terribly depressed. I wondered why Grandmother was living in the basement, which was drafty and damp. Goo Ma was of the educated elite who, like high party members, enjoyed excellent salaries and many privileges. Why should Grandmother be allowed to live in the basement when Goo Ma could afford better quarters?

"Who's there?"

I rushed to her side. "It is me, Grandmother. I received your letter and came as soon as I could."

"Sansan, Sansan, I am so glad to see you. I have much to tell you. Things you must know. Ever since I have been sick I have worried about you and wondered about my duty to you. I thought that if I should die before I had a chance to tell you, you might discover the secret from people who would not tell you all the truth. Or you might never know the secret, and then you would never know your real name."

She held my hands in hers and continued to speak in a little voice.

"Sansan, you are truly my granddaughter. Your father is my second son. Your mother is Mama's elder sister. You are a Chang, not a Soo. Do you understand what I am saying?"

I nodded.

"In 1946 when you were only a few months old, your father was sent to America by his employer. He had to go

alone and leave the family behind because of tight travel restrictions that existed after the war. After six months, he hoped
you all could join him in America.

"But in those difficult times after the war, your parents decided that your mother could bring only one child with her.
Ships going to America were overcrowded and often took over
a month to cross the ocean. And most importantly, they
thought your father's assignment would be for only a year or
two and, by the time of his return, the small children would
hardly have missed their parents.

"Therefore they decided to take only the oldest, your sister
Bei-yee, who was eight. Up until the last minute, your mother
was going to leave your second sister, Kwei-yee, then barely
four, and you, just one, in the care of her sister and her brother-
in-law. But Kwei-yee was old enough to understand and she
began to cry and fuss about being left behind. Second sister's
tears persuaded your mother to make a last-minute decision
and take Kwei-yee along too. Your mother's heart wanted to
take you along most of all because you were her baby, but she
thought the separation would be short and you were so small.
She arranged for her sister, Mei, whom you have always called
"Mama," to make a temporary home for you.

"No one at that time, so close to the end of the World War
—after seven years of bitter fighting against the Japanese—
thought that another war, between the Communists and Na-
tionalists, would break out. But the fighting did start and soon
the situation was deadly serious, and your mother wrote Mei
to ask if she and her husband wanted to leave the mainland and
bring you to Taiwan. But at the time, Mei thought the change
of government not so serious and declined to move. After 1949
and the establishment of Mao Tse-tung and the People's
Republic, it was impossible either for your parents to return or
for you to leave.

"Because of your father's work in the United States, you
were adopted by Mei, and for your safety your name was

changed from Chang to Soo. Mei couldn't have any children and wanted you to be her own. They decided to keep your real identity a secret."

Grandmother paused and leaned her small face forward.

"Sansan, I was also afraid that if I did not tell you the truth now, you might later hear an unkind explanation of what actually happened when you were a baby and perhaps it would turn your heart against your true family. Your mother and father could not foresee the circumstances that eventually separated you and them. In their letters to me, they always ask about you, and I know that they think of you every day and are heartsick about this fate. They send money and food and clothing to all of us, whenever they can without arousing suspicion. Many of those Hong Kong packages that your house and ours have been receiving have come from them. Sansan, you have never left their hearts. Do you understand what I have told you?"

"Yes, Grandmother."

"I hope your heart will receive this news and your parents. I pray you will not resent them."

"Grandmother, I could not resent them, and in a strange way I guess I have always known this secret. Sometimes when I fight with Mama, she yells, 'Go, get out if you want to; you are not a part of this family anyway!' Now that I know who I am, I want to write to my real mother. Can you give me her address?"

"Call my daughter. She can write English. Tell her I want to see her."

"I went upstairs and got Goo Ma, who was correcting some of her students' papers. She came with me to the cellar.

"Daughter, Sansan wants to write to her mother in America. Please address some envelopes for her."

"Mother, I don't think it is wise. If Sansan causes suspicion, we can get into trouble with the authorities."

Grandmother spoke out quickly. "A daughter has the right

to know her own mother. You just write those envelopes, daughter. I will take the responsibility for trouble."

I could see that Grandmother was as stubborn as ever. Goo Ma told me she would have the envelopes ready for me when I left, and went upstairs.

"Sansan," said Grandmother. "Have your mother send her letters here; then Mama won't know about them. You have to be careful not to hurt her."

I agreed, and Grandmother answered my questions about my real family. She showed me some letters and old photographs, and I was proud that the beautiful and happy faces belonged to my mother and father.

That night I secretly wrote my first letter to my parents, and in a month I went to see Grandmother again. Hidden in the seam of her mattress was a letter from Mother to me. I read the letter aloud to Grandmother, who could neither read nor write, and we both cried. I was excited to hear about my real family. My eldest sister had finished graduate studies and my second sister was just starting college. It was a short letter, carefully worded for possible censorship, but filled with warmth and love. When I finished reading it, Grandmother wanted to hear it again. Our tears were happy ones, yet filled with great longing.

From then on, I tried to visit Grandmother at least once a month. During my visits we read letters from my mother, and they made me feel a part of a close and loving family. I had found someone to talk to, someone who cared about me, unlike Mama and Papa who had lost interest in me many years ago. Mother was curious about everything I did and everything I thought. When I read about her concern about my future, my hopes for college would be momentarily rekindled, but I knew well that such hopes were impossible. Still, the letters continued to focus on my future.

On my seventeenth birthday, March 6, I wrote another letter.

Dearest Mother,

Today is my birthday, and I hope there will be a letter from you. I am now seventeen. Enclosed is a picture of me. I want to see if you think I look grown up. Tonight Mama will take me to a restaurant to celebrate, and, in addition, I will get an extra piece of the chocolate candy you sent to the family. Mama, Papa, and I have decided on a rule: every week, each one is allowed two pieces of candy and a glass of powdered milk. With these things you have given us, my life is very full and I am content.

I will graduate very soon. By summer vacation I shall begin to teach. I really wish to change schools, but there's no way. I am now determined to go to night school after I start teaching and make up the subjects for a high-school diploma; and then I shall hope for an opportunity to take the examinations for college. You must know, Mother, that if anything could be done about changing schools, I would do it eagerly.

The last few days I haven't been feeling well; I am running a fever, but the doctors can't find anything wrong. My stomach also ached until I almost cried, but I want you to think of me as an adult now, so I did not.

Mama and Papa have not been getting along lately. Mama's temper is awful. Early each morning she starts with me and then continues with Papa. She never stops. Of course, I know her bad temper is because of her illness; but I also feel that she no longer thinks of me as before. Every week she builds up her anger at me until she yells, "If you don't like home, live at school. Or just die, no one cares!" Whenever she screams like that at me, my heart is deeply wounded. Papa looks on, afraid to say anything.

You might think that I haven't been a good daughter, that I haven't done my chores or studied hard. But I promise, Mother, this is not so. I take care of everything around the house, including doing the laundry, chopping wood, and chipping coals. But still Mama yells. How I wish we could meet. Then I could free my stomach of all the hurts I have swallowed silently in these years. As soon as I can speak to you, I know I shall feel so much better.

Every day I look at your pictures. Since I was too young to remember your faces, I want to memorize you from the photographs.

Please tell First Sister and Second Sister and Father that I love them very much and think of them always.

Since we are separated by thousands of miles, only through your letters can I know what you are doing and thinking. Therefore, please write to me often.

Your loving third daughter,

Sansan

The night of my birthday, I dreamed I was with my family. Mother had baked me a cake, just like the one Kwei-yee had on her birthday. The cake had seventeen candles on it, as was the custom in America.

I did not receive a letter from Mother for the next few weeks. I worried and kept writing, asking her to reply. Finally, in late March, I received bad news.

". . . Sansan, recently my health has not been good. The doctors have advised me to have an operation and suggested that I go to a specialist in Japan. I am now in Tokyo at the hospital and will probably be operated on within a week."

Terrified, I cried until I was empty of the smallest sigh. I prayed to the fates that Mother would be well. Operations are serious, and I was scared for all of us. My heart beat so hard that I thought it would jump out.

I don't know how I lived through the next two weeks. I couldn't tell Mama or Papa because I was still writing in secret. Somehow I continued to go to school and to do my chores at home. But whenever I was in my room alone, I cried and prayed.

Still wrestling with fears, I waited for further news. In late April, I received the third letter from Tokyo. Mother wrote that her health had greatly improved, but that the doctors advised her to rest for another few months. She therefore planned to go to nearby Hong Kong and stay with one of our distant relatives. Mother needed me and wanted me to help her get well. She hoped that I could ask permission to visit her in Hong Kong during my summer vacation.

Grandmother was as excited as I was. She and I seemed to cry whenever I received a letter, but this time we were also laughing. I hugged my small grandmother and our hearts danced.

Grandmother said, "Child, you realize that once you meet your mother, she will bundle you off to America. She does not write of such dreams because of the censors, and she wants you to apply for permission for a visit. But once you are with her in Hong Kong, she will bring you home to your real family."

I had hoped that was the hidden meaning of the letter, and I walked home with plans of how I would nurse Mother back to health.

The very next day I went to the Safety Bureau to see an official about applying for a pass to Hong Kong. I explained the full situation and brought Mother's three letters from Tokyo for verification. The man listened and said, "First you have to get an identification card from your school. Get that and then come back to see us."

I went immediately to see my supervising teacher and repeated my story to him. He warned me that an answer might take a while because the school principal had to get the approval of the Education Bureau.

I had done as much as I could, and now I could only wait. School activities were very demanding, for it was getting closer to final examinations. In addition to studying in every free moment, our class was assigned to planting new trees around the school. On the third day of planting, I felt ill and the doctor gave me an official excuse from school for ten days. Later he had to renew it four times because I burned with fever for forty days.

How did I ever live through the strain of those waiting days? I worried about getting official identification. What if I couldn't get the papers? What if I was too sick to go to see the officials? What if I failed my final examinations? That would surely spoil any plans for visiting Mother, since the officials would never give a poor student any special considerations. I had to take care of myself in the midst of these worries. No one was home during the day, and I had to cook and clean as before.

One night in June, toward the end of my illness, when I had already gone back to my classes, we had just finished supper and I was about to return to my room when Mama said that she wanted to talk with me. She took a letter nervously from her pocket.

"Sansan, I have received a letter from my elder sister. She has told me about your letters to her and her letters to you. Papa and I have talked this over and decided that I should speak to you."

I looked directly at her as she continued.

"When my sister was leaving for the United States, she asked me to take care of you. To tell you the truth, Sansan, I didn't want to. After all, raising a child is not easy. But she was my own sister and I could not refuse. After you came to live with us, Papa and I both grew to love you very much and wanted you to be our own child. So when the revolution started and my sister did not come back to get you, we changed your name and have raised you as ours."

Her voice was unsteady as she spoke, and I knew she was about to cry.

"We've given you everything we could for seventeen years, and now you want to leave us. Didn't we love you and care for you? I know I have a bad temper, but you know, dear, it is because I am not well. We are not young. Papa is almost sixty-five and I am in my late forties. We need you. You needed us when you were small, and we cared for you. Now we are getting old, and we need you. When we adopted you, we thought we could count on you, that you would care for us in our old age. Don't go, Sansan, I beg of you. Give this plan up. Don't go."

Mama was hysterical, and her tears had soaked her dress. I didn't move or say anything but waited until she finished crying. Her wailing was pitiful, but my heart was not moved. I only thought that she did not want me to go because she wanted me to be her insurance for her old age.

Finally, when she calmed down, I said, "Mama, I will always do my duty to take care of you. You have my promise, but if I remain in Tientsin I have no future. As an elementary school teacher I would receive thirty-two yuan a month—not enough to feed myself, much less any family. If I ever get to Hong Kong, perhaps I shall have a chance to go to college. Nothing between is changed if I go; every child has to leave home sometime."

Mama didn't understand and only started to wail again. "Sansan, we raised you and you belong to us. You belong to us."

I knew that no matter what I could say, she would not understand. To her I was and always would be someone who belonged to her or to someone else. She would never understand that I belong to myself.

*   *   *

When Sansan applied for a visitor's pass to Hong Kong, she was closely questioned by Chinese bureaucrats, but after several delays the pass was finally issued. It was a moment never to be forgotten when she was reunited with her mother, and another joyful reunion took place several weeks later at New York's International Airport, where she met other members of her family. In her new home she set to work to improve her English so she could enter college. Her book was written with the help of her sister, Mrs. Winston Lord.

"She is ever mindful," said Mrs. Lord, "of those less fortunate friends she has left behind. While she is sometimes awed by the future, she is secure in the knowledge that at least it is her own."

Sansan, after her graduation from a university near Boston, found a good position with an insurance company. In 1971 travel and trade restrictions between the United States and mainland China were partially lifted. Some observers expressed the hope that eventually the old-time friendship between the peoples of the two countries would be renewed.

16

Refugees from Greece

Poets have sung of "the glory that was Greece," and American thinkers have long been inspired by the ancient Greeks' philosophy about man's right to freedom. When, in 1821, after four hundred years under Turkish rule, the Greeks revolted, philhellenes (friends of Greece) were deeply stirred. Many high-spirited young men both in England and America joined the Greek forces to help them win their independence. Greek orphans rescued by American soldiers and missionaries were sent to the United States for adoption, and a number of them grew up to be distinguished citizens. One was a member of the Wilkes Expedition that explored the Antarctic. One served in the United States Congress. Others became teachers, writers, and ministers.

Although Greece, after eight years of hard fighting, finally won its independence, the next century and a half was a troubled time. The rugged mountains and arid islands of this beautiful country had few natural resources, and the poverty and discontent of a proud people led to frequent political upheavals. In the early part of World War II the country was invaded by the forces of Mussolini, the Italian dictator. Though greatly outnumbered, the Greeks fought valiantly and the Italians were forced to retreat. Not until the Nazis moved in with their powerful tanks and planes was Greece conquered, and the population lived through several years of terror under Nazi occupation.

By 1944 Allied victories had forced the Nazis to leave, but the Greek people were seriously divided. Civil war broke out between Communist guerrillas and guerrillas who supported the government, but the takeover of the country by Communists was finally thwarted. By 1950 they had been defeated, with American assistance in the form of financial aid and military advice. Yet seventeen years later the supposed "threat" of a Communist uprising was given as the excuse for the coup of April 21, 1967, by a junta, or group, of Rightist army colonels. Greece, which had been victimized by Fascists, Nazis, and Communists in turn, now became the victim of another brutal dictatorship, when several units of the Greek army, with tanks and armored cars, suddenly took over all the government offices. The king with his family fled the country, and political enemies of the junta were jailed and frequently tortured. Freedom of speech and other individual liberties, though guaranteed by the Greek constitution, were abolished. Anyone who dared to voice disapproval of the military lived under threat of arrest, including some of the country's most gifted citizens. Mikis Theodorakis, the composer who wrote the score for such well-known movies as *Z* and *Never on Sunday*, spent several years in prison. Other Greeks chose exile abroad, including the popular actresses Irene Pappas and Melina Mercouri.

Soon after the junta seized power, a strict censorship was imposed on the press. Under these circumstances Mrs. Helen Vlachos, an important publisher, suspended publication. Her father, from whom she had inherited a newspaper, had resisted cooperation with the Nazis, and she was equally determined to oppose Colonel George Papadopoulos, leader of the junta.

Since her name was one to be reckoned with in Greece, the colonel was anxious for the cloak of respectability that her approval would provide. But in spite of the pressures brought to bear on her, Mrs. Vlachos refused to resume publishing under censorship, and in an interview with a foreign journalist she referred to the members of the junta as "mediocre men." This was more than the new masters of Greece could take, and she was charged with "insulting the authorities" and refusing to obey a military order that banned criticism of the regime. She and her husband, Costa Loundras, a naval hero of World War II, were placed under house arrest in the couple's penthouse apartment on Mourouzi Street.

After a few days Captain Loundras was permitted to come and go at will, and a maid came in each morning. But to try to prevent Mrs. Vlachos from leaving, a guard was posted outside the apartment door and another stood outside the building. "House Arrest" is condensed from a chapter in the book of that title.

House Arrest (1969)

BY HELEN VLACHOS

"You have to get out of Greece. . . . In the last war, you stayed in Greece and I went and fought and came back and liberated you. Now you go out and do the same."

The most thrilling aspect of this decision was that it was taken by the most conservative of men, Costa, my husband. . . . The very next day the whole operation was accelerated. And the decision was taken. It would have to be tomorrow. Friends had found where to take me, a small basement flat with a telephone securely unknown and untapped. On my last day home, on the eve of the great adventure. I had very little to do. Nothing reminded me of past travel preparations: the only thing I had to pack was myself and a handbag. I tried to see how many jumpers and blouses I could put on one on top of another, in shoplifter's style. But that was about all, as I had to get out of the house dressed in everyday clothes so that if I was caught I could simply say that I was fed up with staying inside and had decided to go for a walk. No suitcases, no guessing what clothes would be needed, no goodbyes, no telephone calls, no last-minute messages to the family, secretary, friends.

We had to think of everything during these last hours. To-night I would be out of the house. I could take nothing with me, and tomorrow I would try to get a suitcase and some clothes from friends, as I could not travel without some luggage. We had also to think of the maid. She would have to be provided with some explanation next morning when she would not find me in the house. "The Kyria felt sick during the night, and we managed to get her secretly out through the back door and take her to her own doctor's nursing home, so as not to go to a prison hospital. You are not to say anything unless you are asked." That was the best we could devise, without hoping for a minute that she would believe it.

Our conversation that day was interspersed with "ifs" and with "don't forgets." "Don't forget to tell the children to write," and "If I get out of Greece safely, remember to send the photographs. And some clothes; I have put the ones I want aside. I will show you. Don't forget the moment I am out to go on making exactly the same noises as if I were still in the house, and don't forget that you must go on pretending that I am inside the house as long as possible."

Then it was Costa's turn.

"Don't forget to be ready to leave the house exactly at the moment we hear the lift going down with the guard. Don't forget to stand on the left of the petrol pump, on Vassilissis Sofia, where the car will be at exactly twenty minutes to eleven. If something goes wrong, which is quite improbable, try to get there on foot. Don't forget the address."

After the maid left, we sat as usual in the living room, reading the foreign newspapers that were full of echoes of the dismal royal adventure. Later, as the time of my departure was approaching, we put both the dogs and the cat under lock and key, took a stroll on the terrace, confirmed that the night was dark and cloudy and quite cold. I tried hard to swallow some dinner. I put a handkerchief over my head, took off my glasses, and wore contact lenses. That was all my "disguise" that night, and I left the flat alone, at twenty past ten. Executing my part of the plan to the minute, I found myself at exactly twenty minutes to eleven standing in Vassilissis Sofia Avenue, near the petrol pump, where there was no car to be seen.

I stood for four and a half interminable minutes on that pavement in the very heart of residential Athens. Scores of friends and acquaintances lived in the neighborhood, and I expected one of them to emerge any minute and to exclaim, full of joyful surprise, "Helen! You are out!"

But the car eventually arrived, and I was whisked to the "hideout" flat and abandoned there for the night. It was cramped, ugly, and bare, miserably furnished. The kitchenette was empty but for a solitary cockroach which scurried away as I came in, and in one of the wall cabinets there were some biscuits, half a bar of chocolate, and nothing else.

I sat wrapped up in my coat, more depressed than at any other time, feeling both miserable and ridiculous. I looked around for something to read and found on a bookshelf in the drawing room half a dozen very dull almanacs and novels. I tried to visualize Costa feeling, probably, just as I felt, all alone in the Mourouzi flat, trying to convey the presence of two people to the guard sitting outside our door by producing all those "familiar noises" that we had written down. He had to put on the radio and the gramophone, call the dogs, open and close doors, run the water in my bath and walk around. Most of the guards were very young men, and the few glimpses they might have had of me must have given them the reassuring picture of a tranquil, white-haired lady.

"I thought it would be quite easy to walk in those high-heeled slippers of yours," Costa said later, "and I put them on to make a realistic tap-tap sound like you did, but I very nearly fell headlong twice as I tripped on the carpet."

Next morning two friends arrived, one by one, "certain of not being followed" in the best spy tradition, and they had brought coffee and sandwiches, and fruit and newspapers. They then returned dutifully to their homes but were back in the afternoon with "everything" ready. "Everything" was a suitcase with some clothes thrown in, collected from friendly feminine wardrobes, as I could not very well get through the customs with nothing but my handbag and a passport accompanied by the necessary police identity card. On both there was a woman's face which resembled mine in that it was the face of another female of the human race. We did not think it mattered much because passport photos are more credible when they do not look like their bearer, but she was a brunette, and something had to be done about that. Either a wig or a dye, and we opted for the second solution as being simpler. A box of Oreal, black, was bought from a central chemist.

By this time it was late afternoon on Saturday, and there was nothing much to be done until Monday morning. I was left alone for the evening. I only hoped that a ticket taking me from anywhere in Greece, by any form of transport, air, ship, or train, to somewhere out of Greece would be secured as quickly as possible, so that I could get away on Monday or Tuesday at the latest.

The next day, Sunday, started and finished as a long briefiing session. Friends and organizers were slinking in and out with ease, as it was the porter's day off.

The subject of the debate was where would I go, what would I do, what would I say? Everyone offered advice, repeated the message I had to give to the free world.

"Look," I said, "let us not hope for much. If I get out of Greece, I will do my best to contact as many people as possible and just tell them the truth, which is bad enough to make any intelligent and honest man turn against the colonels. But if the Greek people themselves don't help, if they just sit and wait for some magic force to shoo the military away, then the junta will stay on, and the subject will just disappear from the foreign press. You know the old cliché: "Dog bites man" is not news, but "man bites dog" is. Well, it does not stop there; it goes on with "man bites dog" is news the first time it happens, and maybe the second, but from then on he can go and swallow a St. Bernard for all the world will care. My telling that these men are ignorant and dishonest, ambitious and dangerous would be just an opinion, not news."

The group was composed of what one would call peaceful people, most of them well established and fairly successful,

certainly not revolutionaries or Communists or even mildly
left-wing. Yet in their bitterness and disappointment they
were finding themselves completely isolated. surrounded by
former allies that could as well have been enemies.

"Look, Helen, you just go and tell them simply: if this situation is allowed to go on, it will eventually deteriorate into civil
war. Helped or not, sooner or later, we will throw the junta
out. . . ."

I let them go on talking, as I was getting tired and confused
and also increasingly anxious about the security of the hideout,
what with the telephone calls and the comings and goings. My
friends were just as worried, and that evening we proceeded
with the hair-dying operation. so that I would have something
in common with the photo in the passport. We read the instructions carefully and emptied the contents of two different
envelopes into a bowl, added water, and stirred. The result, a
thick yellowish mixture, did not look as if it could dye anything
black, and with a toothbrush in hand, we applied more and
more of it. A little later, we were assured of success, as my hair
was getting blacker by the minute. But this success was soon
to be followed by disaster. Not only my hair but my face was
taking on a new look. Evil black patches were appearing all
over my forehead, my ears, my neck.

"Now we have gone and done it. You will never get through
Health Control. You look like a leper."

We had passed half the night putting the hair dye on, and
we spent the rest of it rubbing it off.

Meanwhile a new complication had risen around the next
day, which happened to be my birthday. Birthdays are not
considered especially important in Greece, where the name
day is the occasion for feasting and presents. But under the
circumstances any pretext was good, and my mother had asked
for permission to have lunch with me [at Mourouzi Street],
with the birthday as an excuse. And permission, unfortunately,
had been granted.

"Your mother was splendid!" a friend told me later. "She came with flowers and a cake, and looked quite calm and happy, and even smiled at the guards."

The friend had also brought me the good news that a seat was booked on an air flight to Central Europe for Mrs. X, and that she was due to leave the next afternoon. Meanwhile they had reserved a room for the night in a hotel near the airport, and I was to go there and lie low until it was time to come out into the open. Someone was going to be at the airport to see if I got away all right, but I was not to try to recognize him or to contact him in any way.

Later that day, I met Costa. This time it was the final parting. As we kissed goodbye, he pressed a little icon of Saint Nicholas into my hand. "Keep him with you. I had him with me all through the war. He saved me from the 'piano.' He is a good and lucky saint."

The "piano" was a macabre joke the Greek naval officers stationed in Alexandria had shared during the war. One of the more hospitable Greek ladies, Kiki Salvago, had in her living room an imposing grand piano, on which she placed in heavy silver frames the photographs of Greek officers lost at sea. As the war progressed, the wish to "keep away from Kiki's piano" did not need any explanation.

From that moment on, I was on my own. I registered at the hotel, told the porter that I was feeling tired and wished to have some dinner sent up to my room, left my passport and identity card so that he could fill in the necessary forms. I had nearly twenty-four hours to wait, but I had no intention of risking any budging from the room.

I did not know what was still in wait for me until the next morning, when a nice young man, a junior porter, brought my passport and papers back and said, "You know, your passport is not in order. If you want to travel. . . ."

If I wanted to travel!

As in most true stories of escape or any other unlawful ad-

venture, there had been a slip. The passport, which was supposed to be in perfect order, was not. An all-important detail
had been overlooked, and "If I wanted to travel," as the young
porter had so innocently put it, I had to see to it immediately.
No, he was very sorry, he could not help me; the regulations
demanded that I should go myself.

"You may be able to have it done and finished in the morning," he explained encouragingly. "Shall I call a taxi for you?"

There was not much that I could do but plunge into decision.
"Please do."

What I wanted more than anything was to quarrel with my
organizers, who had never stopped warning me to be careful,
not to make mistakes, not to forget this, and not to overlook
that, and who had let me in, at the very last moment, for
getting right back into the city and trying to put a fake passport in order. But there was nothing else I could do. I either
had to crawl back to Mourouzi Street or give it a try.

A short drive took me to the given address, an imposing
building in the center of the town, crowded with hundreds of
compatriots, with regular police strolling everywhere, and
probably quite a few "Security" around. I went to the information desk, stated my problem, and was told to go and queue at
another department. There, after quite a wait, I got a whole
mass of forms to fill in and sign. Name, parents, date of birth,
profession, children. It was not the first time I had looked at
the passport, and I was familiar with "my" biographical details,
but there were gaps, and there was the problem of the signature which I had not envisaged. Hesitant at first, I grew more
confident with every new form, and I finished by signing with
ease and flourish.

But I got into trouble more than once.

"When did you last travel, Mrs. X?"

When had that woman traveled—or had she? I grabbed the
passport back, turned the pages, and showed him some past
visas with an idiotic smile. There, he could see for himself.

I finished with one department and queued in another. I was terrified of being recognized. By some miracle, during more than three hours I did not see one familiar face.

At one moment the question of foreign exchange arose. I was taking very little in the erroneous belief that the less money you had with you the less suspicious you looked. That was one more mistake. The clerk who noticed this, a nice old Greek, was not in the least suspicious, but just a bit worried. Would I have enough to live on? And how would I get back, seeing that I had no return ticket? I did a lot of explaining, talking of rich relatives who had invited me to be their guest, and this reassurance, together with the long line of people waiting in front of his desk, decided him. In a few minutes I had my passport signed, sealed, and stamped, together with a "Bon voyage."

"You see, it was not very difficult," the young porter said, probably wondering why women make such mountains out of molehills.

"No, it was not, you were quite right."

I thanked him and tipped him much less than I felt like, to keep in character. The morning's ordeal had one good result. Three whole hours passed in the very middle of the crowded Greek offices had reassured me that this dowdy, heavily muffled woman, pale and drawn, with the raven black hair back-combed into a wild-looking nest, was a person who did not look like anybody anyone had ever seen before.

Later I learned that the friendly spy sent to witness my departure was amazed at the ease with which I sailed through all the formalities, answering quickly at the call of my new name, signing forms, looking the clerks right in the eyes. "It was true that I had to look twice myself to recognize her. She looked so awful!" he announced to the very proud and very relieved organizers.

I breathed freely for the first time in days only when I was airborne.

And then I had to fight conflicting emotions. Freedom, in its most intoxicating form, had suddenly been thrust upon me. After having almost none, I was now freer than ever before in my whole life, without definite destination, without appointments, without schedules, without people to see, jobs to do, family responsibilities, ties. Anxiety for the people back home brought a wave of remorse, but at the moment I could not help a reaction of pure glee, a feeling of "having made it." I could not help but think of the police still stolidly sitting outside our door, guarding me in Mourouzi Street, while I was flying over Europe.

During the flight, I pretended to think once again about where I was eventually going, considering Paris, Rome, New York, when I knew all the time in the back of my mind that it was to be London. If one wanted to speak to the Western world, English was the language to do it in, and as a center of communication, London was unbeatable. The BBC was the world's best-heard radio voice, and what's more it spoke four times a day to Greece, in Greek.

For me there was an additional reason, and that was simply that I loved London. When the plane landed at an unfamiliar airport, I went directly to inquire about schedules.

"You can make it if you hurry," the man at the desk said. "There is a plane leaving for London in twenty minutes."

It was dark and very cold when we arrived in London. In the bus riding from the airport to the city I marveled at the lights and the colors; and then, seeing a decorated tree, I realized for the first time that Christmas was only a few days away.

Only last year I would have been deep in preparations, sorting out the presents for the family, personnel, and friends, sending last-minute messages and Christmas cards, decorating the Christmas trees in the offices and at home, organizing family gatherings and festivities, worrying about the Christmas issues of the newspapers and the social activities of both Christmas and New Year.

It was a measure of how much life had changed for me, that this year, for the first time in my life, I had forgotten Christmas.

*   *   *

After Mrs. Vlachos went into exile she wrote about Greece's plight in articles for European magazines and newspapers and made speeches and radio talks. In Greece she had been a leading conservative and a wealthy business woman. The fact that she had taken a great financial loss when she closed down her newspapers and the unusual circumstances of her escape caused one student group to ask how she could call herself a conservative. "Because I wanted to conserve my independence," she replied.

During her years as an editor, Mrs. Vlachos had been a frequent visitor to the United States. After the publication of her book, *House Arrest,* she returned to address the American Association of Newspaper Editors meeting in San Francisco.

17

Escapees from Cuba

Cuba, the beautiful island ninety miles off the shores of the United States, has long been a troubled country. The economy has depended on one crop, sugar, which meant a scarcity of labor during harvest and unemployment and poverty for the masses of people the rest of the year. Conditions worsened after Fulgencia Batista, an army sergeant, seized power through a coup in 1952 and then for several years ruled as dictator. His authority was challenged by an eloquent young lawyer, Fidel Castro, who became the leader of the revolutionists determined to set Cuba free. For several years they waged guerrilla warfare in the Sierra Maestro Mountains before Batista was forced out of office and fled the country.

"Right after the downfall of Batista in the last days of 1958, we were all overjoyed with Fidel's victory," said Juana Castro, his sister, "and filled with such hopes for the future that there was no room for doubts. I remember the day I set out with some friends to meet Fidel on his triumphal march to Havana. . . . The sight of Fidel amid the happy crowds was magnificent. All I thought of then was that the cherished dreams of the revolution were about to flower."

Juana was soon disillusioned about her brother's intentions, as were thousands of other Cubans, including many of the men who had fought under him to free their island from Batista's rule. They were shocked when many of Castro's political enemies were imprisoned and a wave of executions took place without fair trial. Instead of the democratic freedoms that had been promised, harsh new laws were passed. The press, television, and radio were put under government control. Farms and business concerns were nationalized without

198

compensation to the former owners, yet the mass of farmers and city workers were still poor. Cuba was rapidly becoming a police state, and early in December, 1961, Castro announced that he had always been a Communist.

This announcement came as a surprise to some of his closest friends—and to his sister. Appalled by what was happening, she helped members of several underground organizations who were now working against her brother, as they had once worked against Batista. Finally, for her own safety, she escaped to Mexico.

She was only one of many. The majority of those who left went first to Miami, in Florida. For a number of years several thousand refugees arrived in Florida every month. The first wave of escapees were Batista sympathizers, mostly wealthy Cubans. They were followed by professional people and blue-collar workers who had once supported Castro. The wealth of talent and skills which the refugees brought with them proved to be America's gain and Cuba's loss, especially in the field of education.

However, Castro did make a significant contribution in eliminating illiteracy. Out of a population of eight million, two million Cubans were enrolled in a free educational system that provided for a student from the time he entered nursery school until he finished college. A serious handicap was the lack of trained teachers, since many of those who might have served with distinction had fled the country. Another handicap, from the point of view of those who left, was that the school system was dominated by the army, with an army officer serving as minister of education. Even small children were indoctrinated with ideas of militarism and Communism.

Other measures were initiated by the new leader to help the people, but the majority remained poor and lived in fear. Workers who would not volunteer to work overtime without extra pay risked imprisonment. According to one escapee it was considered a crime to criticize the government, and those who did were liable to arrest. Life under such conditions seemed intolerable to the hundreds of thousands who wanted to leave.

In 1965 a list was made up of those residents of the island who would be permitted to fly to Florida—a list that excluded young men of draft age and those engaged in important occupations. In the beginning preference was given those Cubans who had relatives in the United States. Passengers on the planes were required to leave all of their possessions behind. All that they were permitted to take with them was one small suitcase and five dollars in cash.

After the refugees arrived at the Miami airport, many of them were dependent on American government welfare grants and aid from private organizations. The majority, though, were too proud to accept welfare any longer than necessary. Once-prosperous business and professional men took jobs as waiters and parking lot attendants or did any other kind of work that they could find. Eventually many of them obtained better positions or started business enterprises of their own. By 1967 the Cubans had paid the United States government more in income taxes than the total amount expended on their behalf.

The heartening news of their success made many of their countrymen still in Cuba only more anxious to get away. If they were not permitted to depart legally, many of them went to desperate lengths to escape. In trying to cross the ninety miles of water that separated them from Florida, they used all kinds of boats, even small skiffs. Some died in the attempt, but others reached safety. None of them showed greater daring than did one teen-age boy, Armando, whose miraculous flight has been described in the following account.

Stowaway (1969)

BY ARMANDO SOCARRAS RAMÍREZ
AS TOLD TO DENIS FODOR AND JOHN REDDY

The jet engines of the Iberia Airlines DC-8 thundered in ear-splitting crescendo as the big plane taxied toward where we huddled in the tall grass just off the end of the runway at Havana's José Martí Airport. For months, my friend Jorge Pérez Blanco and I had been planning to stow away in a wheel well on this flight, No. 904—Iberia's once-weekly, nonstop run from Havana to Madrid. Now, in the late afternoon of June 3, 1970, our moment had come.

We realized that we were pretty young to be taking such a big gamble; I was seventeen, Jorge sixteen. But we were both determined to escape from Cuba, and our plans had been carefully made. We knew that departing airliners taxied to the end of the 11,500-foot runway, stopped momentarily after turning around, then roared at full throttle down the runway to take off. We wore rubber-soled shoes to aid us in crawling up the wheels and carried ropes to secure ourselves inside the wheel well. We had also stuffed cotton in our ears as protection against the shriek of the four jet engines. Now we lay sweating with fear as the massive craft swung into its about-face, the jet blast flattening the grass all around us. "Let's run!" I shouted to Jorge.

We dashed onto the runway and sprinted toward the left-hand wheels of the momentarily stationary plane. As Jorge began to scramble up the 42-inch-high tires, I saw there was not room for us both in the single well. "I'll try the other side!" I shouted. Quickly I climbed onto the right wheels, grabbed a strut, and, twisting and wriggling, pulled myself into the semi-dark well. The plane began rolling immediately, and I grabbed some machinery to keep from falling out. The roar of the engines nearly deafened me.

As we became airborne, the huge double wheels, scorching hot from takeoff, began folding into the compartment. I tried to flatten myself against the overhead as they came closer and closer; then, in desperation, I pushed at them with my feet. But they pressed powerfully upward, squeezing me terrifyingly against the roof of the well. Just when I felt that I would be crushed, the wheels locked in place and the bay doors beneath them closed, plunging me into darkness. So there I was, my five-foot-four-inch 140-pound frame literally wedged in amid a spaghettilike maze of conduits and machinery. I could not move enough to tie myself to anything, so I stuck my rope behind a pipe.

Then, before I had time to catch my breath, the bay doors

suddenly dropped open again and the wheels stretched out into their landing position. I held on for dear life, swinging over the abyss, wondering if I had been spotted, if even now the plane was turning back to hand me over to Castro's police.

By the time the wheels began retracting again, I had seen a bit of extra space among all the machinery where I could safely squeeze. Now I knew there *was* room for me, even though I could scarcely breathe. After a few minutes, I touched one of the tires and found that it had cooled off. I swallowed some aspirin tablets against the head-splitting noise and began to wish that I had worn something warmer than my light sport shirt and green fatigues.

Up in the cockpit of Flight 904, Captain Valentín Vara del Rey, forty-four, had settled into the routine of the overnight flight, which would last eight hours and twenty minutes. Takeoff had been normal, with the aircraft and its 147 passengers, plus a crew of 10, lifting off at 170 m.p.h. But, right after lift-off, something unusual had happened. One of three red lights on the instrument panel had remained lighted, indicating improper retraction of the landing gear.

"Are you having difficulty?" the control tower asked.

"Yes," replied Vara del Rey. "There is an indication that the right wheel hasn't closed properly. I'll repeat the procedure."

The captain relowered the landing gear, then raised it again. This time the red light blinked out.

Dismissing the incident as a minor malfunction, the captain turned his attention to climbing to assigned cruising altitude. On leveling out, he observed that the temperature outside was 41 degrees F. Inside, the pretty stewardesses began serving dinner to the passengers.

Shivering uncontrollably from the bitter cold, I wondered if Jorge had made it into the other wheel well and began thinking about what had brought me to this desperate situation. I thought about my parents and my girl, María Esther, and wondered what they would think when they learned what I had done.

My father is a plumber, and I have four brothers and a sister. We are poor, like most Cubans. Our house in Havana has just one large room; eleven people live in it—or did. Food was scarce and strictly rationed. About the only fun I had was playing baseball and walking with María Esther along the seawall. When I turned sixteen, the government shipped me off to vocational school in Betancourt, a sugar-cane village in Matanzas Province. There I was supposed to learn welding, but classes were often interrupted to send us off to plant cane.

Young as I was, I was tired of living in a state that con-trolled *everyone's* life. I dreamed of freedom. I wanted to become an artist and live in the United States, where I had an uncle. I knew that thousands of Cubans had got to America and done well there. As the time approached when I would be drafted, I thought more and more of try-ing to get away. But how? I knew that two planeloads of people are allowed to leave Havana for Miami each day, but there is a waiting list of eight hundred thousand for these flights. Also, if you sign up to leave, the government looks on you as a *gusano*—a worm—and life becomes even less bearable.

My hopes seemed futile. Then I met Jorge at a Havana baseball game. After the game we got to talking. I found out that Jorge, like myself, was disillusioned with Cuba. "The system takes away your freedom—forever," he com-plained.

Jorge told me about the weekly flight to Madrid. Twice we went to the airport to reconnoiter. Once a DC-8 took off and flew directly over us; the wheels were still down, and we could see into the well compartments. "There's enough room in there for me," I remember saying.

These were my thoughts as I lay in the freezing darkness more than five miles above the Atlantic Ocean. By now we had been in the air about an hour, and I was getting light-headed from the lack of oxygen. Was it really only a few hours earlier that I had bicycled through the rain with Jorge and hidden in the grass? Was Jorge safe? My parents? María Esther? I drifted into unconsciousness.

The sun rose over the Atlantic like a great golden globe, its rays glinting off the silver-and-red fuselage of Iberia's DC-8 as it crossed the European coast high over Portugal. With the end of the 5,563-mile flight in sight, Captain Vara del Rey began his descent toward Madrid's Barajas Airport. Arrival would be at 8 A.M. local time, the captain told his passengers over the intercom, and the weather in Madrid was sunny and pleasant.

Shortly after passing over Toledo, Vara del Rey let down his landing gear. As always, the maneuver was accompanied by a buffeting as the wheels hit the slipstream and a 200-m.p.h. turbulence swirled through the wheel wells. Now the plane went into its final approach; now, a spurt of flame and smoke from the tires as the DC-8 touched down at about 140 m.p.h.

It was a perfect landing—no bumps. After a brief post-flight check, Vara del Rey walked down the ramp steps and stood by the nose of the plane waiting for a car to pick him up, along with his crew.

Nearby, there was a sudden, soft plop as the frozen body of Armando Socarras fell to the concrete apron beneath the plane. José Rocha Lorenzana, a security guard, was the first to reach the crumpled figure. "When I touched his clothes, they were frozen as stiff as wood," Rocha said. "All he did was make a strange sound, a kind of moan."

"I couldn't believe it at first," Vara del Rey said when told of Armando. "But then I went over to see him. He had ice over his nose and mouth. And his color . . ." As he watched the unconscious boy being bundled into a truck, the captain kept exclaiming to himself, "Impossible! Impossible!"

The first thing I remember after losing consciousness was hitting the ground at the Madrid airport. Then I blacked out again and woke up later at the Gran Hospital de la Beneficencia in downtown Madrid, more dead than alive. When they took my temperature, it was so low that it did not even register on the thermometer. "Am I in Spain?" was my first question. And then, "Where's Jorge?" (Jorge is believed to have been knocked down by the jet blast while trying to climb into the other wheel well, and to be in prison in Cuba.)

Doctors said later that my condition was comparable to that of a patient undergoing "deep freeze" surgery—a delicate process performed only under carefully controlled conditions. Dr. José María Pajares, who cared for me, called my survival a "medical miracle," and, in truth, I feel lucky to be alive.

A few days after my escape, I was up and around the hospital, playing cards with my police guard and reading stacks of letters from all over the world. I especially liked one from a girl in California. "You are a hero," she wrote, "but not very wise." My uncle, Elo Fernández, who lives in New Jersey, telephoned and invited me to come to the United States to live with him. The International Rescue Committee arranged my passage and has continued to help me.

I am fine now. I live with my uncle and go to school to learn English. I still hope to study to be an artist. I want to be a good citizen and contribute something to this country, for I love it here. You can smell freedom in the air.

I often think of my friend Jorge. We both knew the risk we were taking, and that we might be killed in our attempt to escape Cuba. But it seemed worth the chance. Even knowing the risks, I would try to escape again if I had to.

Thank You, America

Americans frequently are given to self-criticism—too frequently, in the opinion of some citizens. Others consider the determination to make right that which is wrong the hallmark of a mature nation. The continuing efforts to realize the ideals of the nation's founders has appealed to thousands of refugees. Because of the contrast between the restrictions they left behind and the possibilities for a new kind of life that have opened up for them, those who sought freedom from persecution on our shores have usually been less concerned with criticism than with appreciation. A number of them have expressed their gratitude in the words, "Thank you, America."

The phrase has had a special meaning for men like Alexander Washchenko. His native Ukraine, like other parts of Eastern Europe, was occupied in turn during World War II by Nazi and Communist forces, and he suffered great hardship before he and his family could be admitted to the United States.

It was night when their ship finally entered New York harbor, and the lights of Manhattan's skyscrapers reminded him of "gigantic Christmas trees." They seemed to hold out "the promise of a radiant future," and he took his wife's hand in his.

"Katryna," he told her, "now we are in America. You and I and the children need never be frightened any more."

The following testament of faith in his adopted country was written in 1955.

* * *

206

Six years now I am living in America. People ask me, "Do you like it here?"

How can I make them understand? Perhaps only someone who, like myself, has tasted the bitterness of life under two totalitarian regimes can fully appreciate how wonderful it is to be free at last. Sometimes I dream that I am back in a Nazi slave-labor camp, or that I am once more doing forced work for the Communists, and I wake up screaming. Before I go back to sleep I pray God to relieve the suffering of the people among whom I was born. And I thank America for permitting me to escape to the freedom of this blessed country.

What has America done for me?

When my wife Katryna and I, with two small children, stepped off the *Marina Marlin* in New York City in 1949, we were strangers in a foreign land. We had no money and no resources and no possessions except the clothes we wore. Today we are rich in friends. We discovered that in America it is the custom to be kind to strangers. In every place where we have lived, our American neighbors have gone out of their way to lend us a helping hand.

By American standards we are hardly rich in material possessions. But I make good money, and I have a job with people I like and respect. We have a good home, wear good clothes, eat good food. We have a telephone, an automobile, a bank account—things which, as a boy in the Ukraine, I never even imagined my possessing. Our children are getting a good education.

This summer I am reserving two evenings a week for my class in citizenship, which meets in the same school my children attend. I realize that becoming a naturalized American is a very serious matter, and I want to make very certain that I pass my examination. I know that the proudest day of my life will be when I can say, "I am a citizen of the United States."

Thank you, America.